FIGHTER!

TEN KILLER PLANES OF WORLD WAR II

JIM LAURIER

VOYAGEUR PRESS

CONTENTS

OBSOLETE— YET IMMORTAL

By Michael Dolan

In Jim Laurier, the aircraft of the golden age of propeller flight find a worthy chronicler, not only in language, but also in image. Jim's extraordinary renderings of ten legendary planes in *Fighter! Ten Killer Planes of World War II* bring alive an era of aerial combat long lost in the contrails of jets and missiles and drowned out by the sinister hum of the drone. World War II fighting planes, once the leading edge of their kind, now stand as quaint relics, their nimbleness and speed and armaments humbled by history and technology's unyielding march.

So in steps Laurier, transporting the reader back to when each of these warbirds was the new thing—revolutionary and pivotal, if only for a blink. With his prose and his pictures he banishes modernity, allowing the reader to appreciate the deadly power and martial precision of planes that soared and dove and banked over a world at war—doomed to obsolescence, yet immortal.

Michael Dolan is editor of American History *magazine. As senior editor of* World War II *(2012–2016), he researched and wrote that magazine's "Weapons Manual" spread, illustrated by the author.*

INTRODUCTION

War, despite its horrific effects, seems an unavoidable necessity from time to time. I once heard a claim that, in all of human history, there has been only a period of one hundred years during which war wasn't raging somewhere on our small planet. If that is a fact, I suppose it gives stark insight to the aggressive nature of our species.

In the late 1930s, war loomed once again, this time on a global scale. When the fuse was lit, the conflict propagated quickly across borders and oceans until every corner of the world was affected. Governments, armies, and civilians were embroiled in the conflict now known as World War II.

As a pilot, I am of course interested in aviation and have been for most of my life. I've drawn pictures of aircraft since about age three. I admire piston-powered airplanes most, and the aviation designs of World War II are of particular interest to me. In my mind, the years 1937 through 1945 were the heyday

of piston-powered flight. During these war years, military technology made astonishing leaps forward, resulting in new war machines of every conceivable configuration.

Like today's jet-powered fighters, combat aircraft of World War II were designed for a lethal purpose, yet they were also aesthetically pleasing in shape and proportion. They were engineering and design marvels, and when we see and hear them lift into the sky today, they capture our imaginations as much as the concept of flight itself.

In *Fighter! Ten Killer Planes of World War II*, I have selected what I consider ten pivotal fighter designs of the period and attempted to explain why, to my mind, they were important in shaping the course of the war. For each, I give a brief outline of its development and operational history, along with some technical specifications. Period photos provide further context.

I created the artworks in this book as paintings in oils or acrylics, as digital images with Photoshop, or with a combination of these methods. They are my interpretations of actual events based on my research. In each case I have tried to remain faithful to the technical accuracy of the aircraft as well as the events and locations of the missions in which they were recorded as being involved.

In creating the artworks that illustrate the words, and which are the essence of this book, I've tried to effectively capture real moments of life-and-death struggle in the skies of World War II. Hopefully these images offer a glimpse of what it looked like in this unique battle arena, and give pause to reflect on how these battles affected not only the lives of those who participated in them, but the lives of all those who anxiously awaited the final outcome.

Regardless of what language the combatants spoke, which country they served, or the era in which they fought, courage, life, and death were the same for each. Any warrior who dares to enter into conflict knowing he or she may have to give their life to save others is worthy of celebration and remembrance. In that spirit, I dedicate this book to all who ever served, and those who currently do.

CHAPTER 1
MESSERSCHMITT
Bf 109

Despite restrictions imposed by the Treaty of Versailles, by the early 1930s Germany was secretly building its aviation arsenal under the guise of developing transport and passenger planes. The aircraft were designed with the unspoken notion of being easily converted to military purposes.

In 1934 Aviation Minister Hermann Göring sent a confidential message to Wilhelm Emil "Willy" Messerschmitt, asking him to develop a lightning-fast, single-seat, low-wing monoplane. What Göring was really asking of Messerschmitt was to design a new front-line fighter, which became the Bf 109. The aircraft's *Bf* designation indicated Bayerische Flugzeugwerke, or Bavarian Aircraft Works, the firm that submitted the original design. The fighter would retain those model letters even after Willy Messerschmitt acquired the company and changed its name in 1938.

Messerschmitt and his design team began design work on the new aircraft, incorporating the new features utilized in their Bf 108 Taifun (typhoon) design, which was used as a four-seat light transport. The Bf 108 had the newest features of the period, including retractable landing gear, an enclosed cockpit, and leading-edge slats and trailing-edge flaps in the wings. One of the Bf 109's most distinctive design features, however, was the location of its guns on the centerline of the airplane, which gave it a tightly focused and lethal cone of fire. With two heavy machine guns on the cowling and one cannon firing through the nose, a short, well-aimed burst could bring down anything in the air, including heavy bombers. The Bf 109's nose-mounted weapons and REVI gunsight more than compensated for any shortcomings in its design.

The new aircraft's first production type, the Bf 109A, entered service in the Spanish Civil War in December 1937 and was soon followed in February and March 1938 by the Bf 109B variants. The new Luftwaffe pilots were formed into the so-called Condor Legion and fought for Gen. Francisco Franco y Bahamonde in opposition to the Republican government. The first few months were difficult for the German pilots as they learned to tame the quirkiness of their new fighters. The biggest problem seemed to be the aircraft's narrow-stance landing gear and its tendency to drop its left wing when power was applied for takeoff, resulting in many ground accidents. The problem was caused by the inverted V-12 engine's torque roll, for which pilots learned to compensate by applying a lot of rudder during takeoff.

The Luftwaffe's initiation into combat with the Bf 109 occurred in the skies above Spain against Soviet pilots flying Polikarpov I-16 fighters, which were a good match for 109s at lower altitudes. However, the Bf 109 was faster in level flight and in dives, and was far superior to the Soviet aircraft above 9,000 feet (2,740m).

The Bf 109's combat service in Spain drove a quick succession of design changes, and the aircraft was continuously improved until the end of World War II; initial successive variants were the 109A, 109B, 109C, and 109D. Then, in 1939, the Bf 109E debuted in Germany's invasion of Poland and played a large role in

The High Tide of Summer. In southern Russia, the vast, gently rolling plains of Ukraine seem to stretch forever. Many German aces were made on the Eastern Front. One of the best was Günther Rall of JG 52. Rall flew against the best the Soviets had to offer and ended the war with 275 victories to his credit, the third highest in history. Rall is depicted climbing into his Messerschmitt Bf 109G 3, *Black 13*, in the late summer of 1942. His *schwarz* men stand by to assist him as he prepares to leave on another sortie over the plains.

PREVIOUS PAGES: Bf 109F-2 flown by Geschwaderkommodore Oberstleutnant Werner Mölders, Stab/JG 51, June 1941.

©Jim Laurier
8·4·92

ABOVE: **Bf 109B number 6-12 of II./J 88**, the second group of the famed Condor Legion, was flown by Hermann Stange. It is shown here at Pontejos-Santander Airfield, Spain, during the Spanish Civil War.

LEFT: ***Mölders Flight.*** Werner Mölders leads a mixed group of Bf 109Es on a mission across the English Channel toward England in mid-August 1940. At the time, Mölders was commandant of II./JG 2, based in Pihen-lès-Guînes, France. He was a rising star in the Luftwaffe, but his life would be cut short when he died in a transport plane crash in 1941.

the Battle of France and the Battle of Britain. In late 1940, Messerschmitt AG tested the F-0 variant, which incorporated a more aerodynamic cowling and air scoop and rounded wingtips. The F-2 that followed featured a higher-velocity MG 151 centerline cannon.

In the late summer of 1942, the first G variant was introduced with a more powerful Daimler-Benz DB 605A engine rated at 1,475 horsepower. Improvements continued among the G variants. The G-5 replaced the aircraft's cowl-mounted MG 17 guns with the two MG 131 guns that gave subsequent Bf 109Gs their distinctive humps, which were fairings needed to cover the guns' larger breech blocks. For this reason, pilots called the new G type the *Beule* ("bump"). Later, the G-10 received a cowl redesign to eliminate the bumps, giving the aircraft a more streamlined shape forward of the firewall.

By 1944, the Bf 109G was showing its age and was outclassed by most contemporary Allied fighters. In an attempt to match performance with the Allies, Messerschmitt AG added nitrous oxide injection to the DB 605D engines in late 1944; some engines were given methanol-injection systems that boosted their horsepower from 1,550 to 2,000. Other design changes included wooden tails and rudders, as well as canopies with less framework for better visibility. These later models could achieve speeds of 428 miles per hour (689kmh) at 25,000 feet (7,620m).

All of these late-war design improvements were attempts to help the Bf 109 gain an edge over, or at least maintain pace with, its Allied counterparts. Despite all the latest innovations, it was a case of too little too late for the Luftwaffe and its main fighter, as dwindling supplies, logistical difficulties, and undertrained pilots made it all but impossible to fight effectively. The fact that the Bf 109 remained a worthy adversary as late in the war as it did was due largely to the skill of the veteran pilots who still flew the type. The three top-scoring aces in history—Erich Hartmann (352 victories), Gerhard Barkhorn (301), and Gunther Rall (275)—achieved most of their victories in the cockpits of Bf 109s.

The final Bf 109 variant was the K, with one MK 108 or MK 103 cannon and two MG 151 cowl-mounted guns. The Bf 109K saw limited combat action, however, serving primarily in January 1945 during the doomed Operation Bodenplatte in the Low Countries.

The Bf 109 would go down as the most-produced fighter aircraft in history, with 33,984 built. And its ominous, low-profile silhouette made it one of the most recognizable aircraft of World War II. With its combination of hard, angular lines and smooth, compound curves, it seemed to be the mechanical embodiment of German society itself, evincing cultural awareness, discipline, and serious intent. A closer look revealed a curious blend of advanced engineering and utilitarian design. When war

came to an end for Germany, and thus the Bf 109, on May 8, 1945, some remained in service in Finland, Switzerland, Spain, and elsewhere.

★ ★ ★

Any pilot who encountered the Messerschmitt Bf 109 in combat could attest that it was not an aircraft to be underestimated in any situation or at any altitude when flown by a competent pilot. But, by late war, many of the Luftwaffe pilot *Experten* had been lost, and new pilots were given only rudimentary training on the type due to fuel shortages and other problems. Losses mounted quickly for the Luftwaffe, regardless of the type of aircraft flown.

Writing in *Aviation History* in 1999, John Guttman noted, "Perhaps [the Bf 109] was not the best performer of the war, and even its pilots would admit that it was not the safest or most comfortable plane to fly.

ABOVE: "Black 12," a Bf 109G-6 of II./JG 2 (Jagdgeschwader 2's second group) shows the R6 gun package in September 1943. The R6 was a bad-weather variant of the G that featured autopilot.

OPPOSITE: *Max Ostermann.* Max Ostermann was a 102-victory ace. He was originally assigned to Zerstörergeschwader (ZG) 1, which was equipped with Messerschmitt Bf 110s, but the group commander noted Ostermann was too small to fly the large twin-engine fighter-bomber and transferred him to JG 21, which flew Bf 109s. Blocks were fitted to the rudder pedals so Ostermann's feet could reach them. He flew in the Battle of France and the Battle of Britain with JG 21 before the unit was redesignated JG 54 and moved to the Eastern Front. In this scene, Ostermann claims a Polikarpov I-15 in January 1942 while escorting Stuka dive-bombers to and from a target in Soviet territory.

RIGHT: A Finnish Bf 109 pilot confers with a fellow airman in June 1944. The Finns used the Bf 109 to great effect against the Soviets, scoring 667 confirmed victories and losing 34 of the 159 they received to enemy fighters or antiaircraft fire.

OPPOSITE: **Steinhoff's Charge.** Around 8:00 a.m. on August 25, 1943, German fighter ace Johannes Steinhoff took off from Foggia Airfield in southern Italy to test a new engine that had been installed in his Bf 109G-6. Oberleutnant Theo Lindemann flew as his wingman. Only a few miles from Foggia, Steinhoff and Lindemann encountered approximately 140 P-38 Lightnings inbound from their bases in North Africa for an early-morning surprise attack on the German airfields in the area. In a head-on pass, Steinhoff fired into the Lightnings, downing two. One of the P-38 pilots bailed out and was captured by the Germans.

FOLLOWING: **Adler Schwarm.** The Luftwaffe's Maj. Günther Rall and twenty-five Messerschmitt Bf 109Gs of II./JG 11 under his command lift off of the airfield in Husted, Germany, on May 12, 1944. They are headed to intercept a large formation of American bombers headed toward Germany, target unknown. The Messerschmitts are to engage the American escort fighters so that the more heavily armed Fw 190s can attack the bombers. In a dogfight with P-47 Thunderbolts of the 56th Fighter Group, Rall would be shot down and made a POW, making this his last combat mission of the war.

But its combat record, from beginning to end, was monumental, and it was the weapon of choice for the greatest fighter pilots in history."

In 1999, Guttman had interviewed Eino Ilmari Juutilainen for *Military History*. Juutilainen holds the distinction of being the top-scoring non-German fighter ace in history. Flying against Soviet pilots in World War II, Juutilainen scored fifty-eight of his ninety-four confirmed victories from the cockpits of Bf 109s. Having transitioned from Brewster B-239s, Juutilainen told Guttman, "I would say that whereas the Brewster was a gentleman's airplane, the Messerschmitt was a killing machine."

Captain Eric Brown was a British Royal Navy pilot and chief officer of captured enemy aircraft who flew a captured Bf 109G in 1944. "The Bf-109 always brought to my mind the adjective 'sinister,'" he wrote in his book *Wings of the Luftwaffe: Flying the Captured German*

Aircraft of World War II. "It has been suggested that it evinced the characteristics of the nation that conceived it, and to me it always looked lethal from any angle, on the ground or in the air; once I had climbed into its claustrophobic cockpit, it felt lethal!"

Heimo Lampi was another Finnish ace (13.5 victories) who flew Bf 109s. "Väinö Pokela was tasked with the mission of teaching us Brewster pilots into Messerschmitts," he told Hannu Valtonen in the latter's book, *Messerschmitt Bf 109 and the German War Economy*. "I made it in just two familiarization flights directly into the Me squadron, but not all did it. Some had to return to Brewsters. After the war I had to teach wing-commander Holm to fly the Messerschmitt. I felt that forcing an old man into this was suicide. But order was order. But I knew how to give orders as well. I told him: 'You don't force this plane up from the runway, but you let it fly off by

Continued on page 22

ABOVE: Flying against Soviet pilots in World War II, Eino Ilmari Juutilainen scored fifty-eight of his ninety-four confirmed victories from the cockpits of Bf 109s.

BELOW: By getting in very close to his enemy, firing, and then diving away while using the Bf 109's powerful engine to swing around for the next attack, Erich Hartmann became the greatest ace of his era with 352 confirmed victories.

Continued from page 19

itself!' The flight succeeded excellently. It was amazing performance from an old man."

In 1990 at a fighter pilot forum at the Champlin Fighter Museum in Mesa, Arizona, I had the opportunity to meet and speak with some Luftwaffe aces, including Ernst Scheufele, who flew Fw 190s and Bf 109s in World War II. He was a lean man, standing slightly over six feet, and appeared too tall to fit into the cockpit of the flyable Bf 109 that was on display. However, he did so with the same ease as he must have as a young pilot. Once in the cockpit, he looked completely at home and even asked in German if the guns were loaded (*Ist die MGs geladen?*). He called the 109 a "strange kite," but said he loved it in combat as much as the Fw 190, each having mostly favorable traits against just a very few on the negative side.

Being six feet tall and 235 pounds, I'm a bit larger than the typical pilot of the 1940s, but I was eager to sit in the 109. I climbed into the cockpit and, without being able to fly it, could formulate at least a limited impression of the airplane. It did feel a bit cramped at my shoulders, which were pressed against the canopy rails on either side. And tilting my head too far to the left or right, I might bump the canopy's side glass, but leaning back, my head could touch the armored plate behind the seat, which must have been reassuring to the pilot. Otherwise, I was surprised that it felt quite comfortable, with the seating position allowing my legs to extend forward to the rudder pedals with very little bend at the knee. And having the legs more or less out straight in a fighter aircraft is an advantage in helping counter the g-forces experienced during combat maneuvers. (A similar seating position can be found in today's fighter jets, including the F-16 Falcon.) It would appear that the Germans took this into consideration when incorporating this feature into their designs.

Moving the Bf 109's control column, I found it had plenty of "throw," with more than adequate movement for all flight maneuvers, though it might hit my legs occasionally. The instrument panel at first glance looked a bit sparse compared to the P-51 Mustang's, for example. But after browsing the cockpit for a few moments, it was apparent that all necessary instruments and gauges were present, arranged logically and ergonomically. Controls on the left and right sides of the cockpit were mostly easy to reach and thoughtfully arranged. The forward armored windscreen at first seemed a bit small, and looking aft right and left as much as I could, the rearward vision was a bit restricted. However, after sitting in the cockpit for a few minutes I was very comfortable, like I had become part of the airplane. My impressions simply sitting in the cockpit must be different than flying it in combat, but apparently it posed little problem for its pilots, given the number of aircraft that fell victim to Bf 109s during the war.

Luftwaffe pilot Günther Rall became third-highest scoring ace in history with 275 confirmed victories, 272 of them on the Eastern Front and 241 against Soviet aircraft. All of his victories were achieved in the Bf 109. Through mutual friends and associates, I became acquainted with Rall in 1992 and over a number of years we worked together on various art projects. He once told me he thought the Bf 109 was easy to fly once you became comfortable with it and he felt it had no real drawbacks. In his opinion, it was a perfect gun platform in the majority of combat situations and a very good match against any adversary. Such comments are typical from fighter pilots who have mastered their aircraft. This may be a result of the pilot becoming very familiar with a particular aircraft rather than the aircraft's actual merits.

The highest scoring ace of all time is Luftwaffe pilot Erich Hartmann (352 confirmed victories). Hartmann attributes his high score to unique tactics he learned while flying as wingman for Walter Krupinski. Speaking to Eric Brown after the war, he stated, "I didn't open fire 'til the aircraft filled my whole windscreen. If I did this, I would get one every time."

Günther Rall scored 275 aerial victories with the Bf 109, most on the Eastern Front against Soviet pilots.

Bf 109s wrecked and abandoned in North Africa. The first fuselage wears the markings of III. *Gruppe* (3rd Group) of a fighter wing, probably III./JG 27. An abandoned Messerschmitt Bf 110 also seems to be visible in the center background.

Interestingly, this was a tactic often used by Manfred von Richtofen (the Red Baron), the highest scoring ace of World War I. By getting in very close, firing, and then diving away and using the Bf 109's powerful engine to swing around for the next attack, Hartmann became the greatest ace of his era. He successfully used his aircraft's strengths to exploit the enemy aircraft's weaknesses—one of the most fundamental air combat principles. Here, the Bf 109 could clearly excel when flown by the right pilot.

Among new pilots, the Bf 109 was preceded by a reputation as being somewhat intimidating to learn to fly. It was rumored to have a cramped cockpit with limited visibility in some directions, tricky ground-handling characteristics on landing and takeoff, and some early structural design weaknesses in the empennage. The leading edge wing slats would deploy in certain flight conditions, creating a "notching" effect felt in the control column—a bit disconcerting to a pilot not accustomed to it. Despite its record, not all Luftwaffe pilots could warm up to the Bf 109—many

preferred the Fw 190 or other aircraft—but once a pilot had mastered its eccentricities and felt comfortable, it became a lethal weapon in skilled hands.

Because the Bf 109 was the most-produced fighter in history, had one of the longest service records of any World War II fighter, and accounted for the greatest combined number of kills, it should be counted among the greatest fighter planes ever built. Perhaps the only real shortcoming of its design was its limited range. Beyond that it was (and still is) a beautiful aircraft to see, on the ground or in the air. Its Daimler-Benz DB 605 engine sounds like no other—music to the ears of any aviation enthusiast fortunate enough to witness it in flight. It had a relatively low-profile fuselage, making it a difficult target to hit. It was fairly light and possessed a powerful and dependable engine and weapons system.

But ultimately, the skill of a pilot is what counts most in aviation. A great fighter can become an amazing fighter with the right pilot, and that is at the core of the Messerschmitt Bf 109's legacy. It was truly a fighter pilot's airplane.

ABOVE: A Bf 109 in Bulgaria in June 1944 uses the aircraft's fuselage humps as an opportunity to incorporate some interesting artwork.

LEFT: **Marauder Mayhem.** Martin B-26 Marauders rarely mixed with Luftwaffe fighters; most bomber losses were due to antiaircraft fire, as the planes usually flew at medium altitudes. However, one fighter encounter occurred on December 23, 1944, when B-26s of the 387th Bomb Group flew a mission to the railroad bridge at Mayen in Germany. For some reason, the low flight lagged behind the rest of the formation, and a group of Bf 109Gs took advantage of the situation, sweeping in for an attack and downing four Marauders in quick succession. Not holding a tight formation was often costly for bombers and their crews.

MESSERSCHMITT
Bf 109

AIRCRAFT DEPICTED

Bf 109G-6

Flown by Hauptmann Gerhard Barkhorn

II./JG 52

August 1943

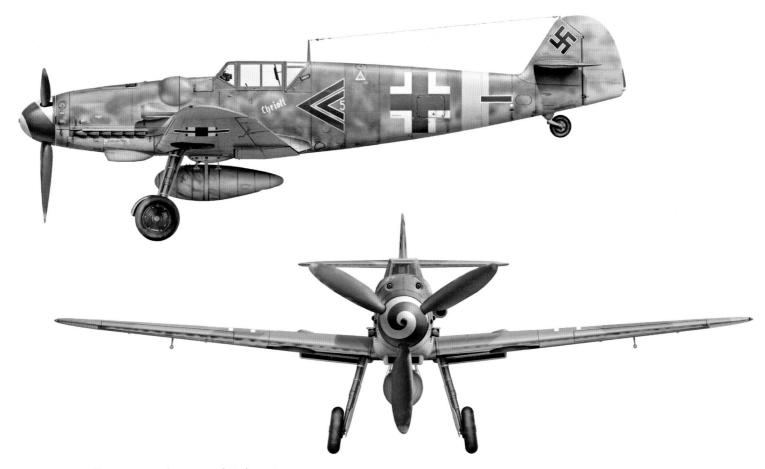

DESIGNERS: Willy Messerschmitt and Robert Lusser
MANUFACTURER: Bayerische Flugzeugwerke AG
AIRFRAMES PRODUCED: 33,984

SPECIFICATIONS

Length . . . . 29 ft 7 in (9.02m)	Maximum speed . . . . 398 mph (640kmh)
Wingspan . . . . 32 ft 7 in (9.93m)	Cruising speed . . . . 370 mph (595kmh)
Height . . . . 10 ft 6 in (3.20m)	Landing speed . . . . 91 mph (146kmh)
Empty weight . . . . .5,000 lb (2,268kg)	Ceiling . . . . 36,745 ft (11,200m)
Loaded weight . . . . .5,906 lb (2,679kg)	Range . . . . .348 mi (560km)
Engine . . . . Daimler-Benz DB 605A-1	Armament . . . . 7.92mm MG 17 machine guns x 2
Output . . . . 1,475 hp	20mm MG 151 cannon x 1

MESSERSCHMITT Bf 109

1. Machine gun firing button safety cover
2. Control column
3. Rudder pedal
4. Fuel cock
5. FuG VII radio control switch
6. Fuel contents gauge
7. Cockpit lamp control knob
8. Pitot head–heating warning lamp
9. Circuit breaker
10. Airspeed indicator
11. Engine starter switch
12. Turn and bank indicator
13. Altimeter
14. Compass
15. Instruction plate for flap settings and landing speed
16. Clock
17. REVI C 12D gunsight
18. Boost gauge
19. Compass deviation table
20. Tachometer
21. Propeller pitch indicator
22. Undercarriage position indicator
23. Double fuel and oil pressure gauge
24. Undercarriage control lever
25. Undercarriage emergency control lever

26. Mechanical undercarriage position indicator

27. Filter pump control lever

28. Coolant temperature gauge

29. Oil temperature gauge

30. Fuel low warning lamp

31. Elevator control wheel

32. Landing flap control lever

33. Oil cooler flap control lever

34. Throttle control lever

35. Main instrument lighting lamp

36. Engine emergency stop hand lever

37. Engine ignition hand lever

38. Starter coupling hand lever

39. Canopy jettison lever

40. Seat height adjustment lever

41. Elevator incidence indicator

42. Electrical circuit breaker panel

43. Oxygen hose

44. Main instrument lighting lamp

45. Radiator flap control handle

46. Fuel pump auto-switch

47. Map holder

48. Pilot's seat

49. Seat harness adjustment lever

50. Fuel injection pump

51. Remote control ventilator

52. Oxygen equipment

CHAPTER 2

HAWKER
Hurricane

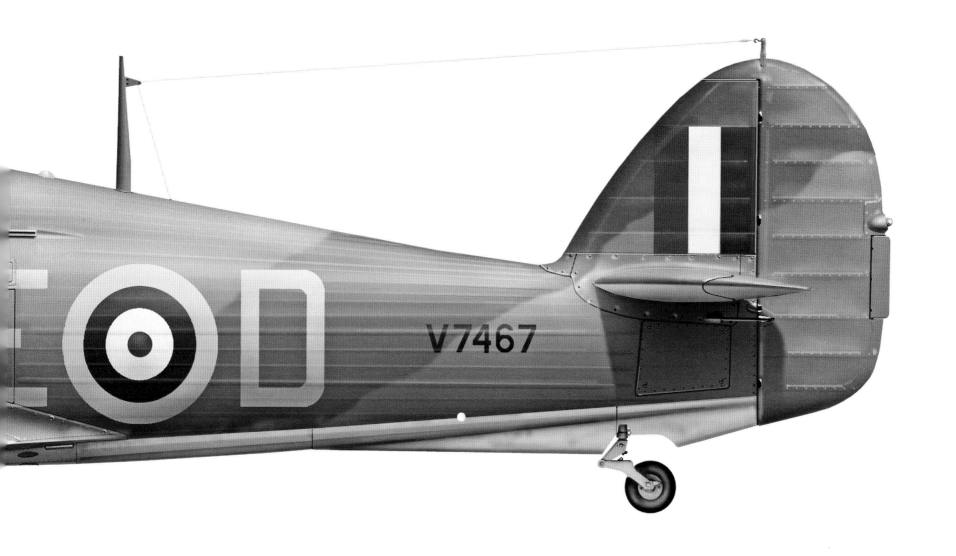

The Hawker Hurricane was the "other" famous front-line fighter put into service by the British Royal Air Force (RAF) in World War II. Along with the Supermarine Spitfire (see Chapter 7), it gained notoriety in the Battle of Britain in the summer of 1940. It was a much simpler design than the Spitfire, but was easier to build and packed a good punch with its closely grouped array of eight machine guns in the wings.

The Hurricane was designed by an engineer named Sydney Camm. Camm worked at Hawker Engineering Company as a senior draftsman until he became chief designer in 1925 and was responsible for a number of aircraft designs in the years leading up to 1934. Two of his successful designs were the metal-and-fabric Hawker Nimrod and Fury biplanes. These two designs would be the basis for the first Hawker monoplane design that Camm had been musing over for a time.

The RAF had many Hawker aircraft in its inventory during the 1930s, and Camm submitted his proposal for a new low-wing fighter in 1934. It was rejected, however, as the Spitfire prototype had already been commissioned. The Spitfire was viewed as a more modern design, and its initial testing had so impressed the Air Ministry that it was deemed sufficient to meet all its fighter requirements.

Undaunted, Camm pursued his monoplane designs as a private venture, making further improvements along the way. As problems arose during the Spitfire's development, the Air Ministry began to show interest in Camm's airplane. On November 6, 1935, Hawker Hurricane prototype K5083 made its first flight with test pilot P. W. S. "George" Bulman at the controls. It weighed only 5,416 pounds and was powered by a Rolls-Royce Merlin C engine. The aircraft was reported to be very stable and easy to fly and had attained a speed of 315 miles per hour (507kmh). Testing continued with impressive results, and the Air Ministry ordered six hundred aircraft in the summer of 1936, with the first production aircraft, the Mk I, flying on October 12, 1937.

The Hurricane Mk I was powered by either a Rolls-Royce Merlin II or III engine; had a either a Watts fixed-pitch, two-bladed wooden propeller or a de Havilland or Rotol three-blade metal prop; and carried eight .303-inch machine guns in the wings. The fuselage aft of the cockpit and the wings were fabric covered. After about the first three hundred aircraft came off the production line, the wings were aluminum clad.

At the outbreak of war, eighteen RAF squadrons had been equipped with a total of 497 Hurricanes, No. 111 Squadron being the first to receive the new fighters. In the Battle of Britain, the Hurricanes were typically used against German bombers, the Spitfires being a bit faster and more maneuverable at higher altitudes where Bf 109s were found flying cover for the bomber formations. But technological advances in newer fighter aircraft designs began outpacing the Hurricane, and the rugged fighter took on other roles to which it was better suited. Subsequently Hurricane development became more focused on fighter-bomber

Shared Victory. Pilot Officer Tom Neil achieved fourteen aerial victories flying the Hawker Hurricane in the Battle of Britain. On September 15, 1940, in one of his 141 combat missions, Neil's No. 249 Squadron was scrambled to intercept an incoming German bomber formation and their Bf 109 fighter escorts. Several Spitfire squadrons had also been scrambled, and a furious air battle ensued. The RAF had lost many of its fighters by this time, and, realizing the stakes were high and the margin for error small, they fought fanatically against the Germans, who as always outnumbered them. Some German bomber crews stated after the battle that British fighters pressed their attacks so close it looked as if they intended to ram the bombers. In fact, in some cases RAF fighters and Germans bombers did collide. Neil, flying his Hurricane Mk I, claimed one Dornier downed and another shared with a Spitfire.

PREVIOUS PAGES: Hawker Hurricane Mk I flown by Squadron Leader Douglas Bader, RAF No. 242 Squadron, September 1940.

OPPOSITE: ***The Lion's Claws.*** In August 1940, a flight of No. 615 Squadron Hurricane Mk Is heads out over the English Channel to intercept an incoming force of German bombers. The near Hurricane is flown by Pilot Officer Anthony Truran. On August 15, Truran was attacked in this aircraft and forced to return to RAF Kenley with leg wounds and a heavily damaged aircraft.

RIGHT: Pilots scramble for their Hurricanes at an airfield in England during the Battle of Britain. In addition to those from Great Britain, pilots from Poland, Czechoslovakia, and Canada helped defend the British Isles.

types and other lower-altitude uses. Its very sturdy construction, heavy firepower, and ability to absorb horrendous punishment made it an ideal choice for this kind of work.

The Hurricane Mk II used the Merlin XX engine, which increased its top speed at medium-high altitudes. The Mk II entered service near the end of the Battle of Britain and saw limited combat in the conflict. The Mk II series was produced in more variants than any other. Mk IIa Series 1 had its fuselage lengthened by 7 inches to accommodate a new engine. Mk IIa 2 had strengthened fuselage and wings and the ability to carry two drop tanks.

The Mk IIb had twelve .303-inch machine guns in total and two bomb racks added to the wings, while the Mk IIc could carry a 20-millimeter Oerlikon cannon

under each wing or two Hispano-Suiza 20-millimeter cannons in each wing. Almost five thousand examples of this type, either produced or converted from Mk IIbs, made it one of the most common variants.

An antitank version called the Mk IId carried two 40-millimeter Vickers cannons under each wing. Armored versions had more protection against ground fire but were slower and more vulnerable to fighter attacks. Unarmored versions were faster but were susceptible to ground fire. Later versions of this type were equipped with rockets instead of guns.

The Mk IIe was meant to be more versatile than the IId in that it used a universal wing design that allowed a variety of weapons to be mounted on the wings depending on the tactical profile required. It saw limited use and was replaced by the Mk IV, which had a more powerful engine.

A photo-recon version of the Hawker called the PR Mk II was introduced in 1942. It was stripped of armament and had extra fuel tanks and cameras installed. Even with these modifications, it lacked enough range to be of great use and was phased out as more capable aircraft became available.

Some Hurricanes were modified for use by the Fleet Air Arm for use in aircraft carrier operations and to protect merchant shipping. A small number of these naval Hurricanes were even modified to be launched off merchant ship catapults when enemy aircraft approached. Once launched, these "Hurricats" or "Catafighters" could not land back on the ship and had to be ditched at sea. Naval Hurricanes saw very limited service. Most were phased out by 1943.

Hurricanes also saw service in several foreign countries, including Argentina, Australia, Belgium, Canada, Czechoslovakia, Egypt, Finland, Free France, Greece, India, Iran, Ireland, Netherlands, New Zealand, Norway, Poland, Portugal, Romania, South Africa, the Soviet Union, Turkey, and Yugoslavia.

Hurricane production reached 14,533 aircraft, the last in 1944 with serial number PZ865. It was retained by the manufacturer for trials work.

★ ★ ★

Though the Hawker Hurricane was developed at the same time as the Spitfire and for the same purposes, they had entirely different design approaches. The Spitfire used new technology, while the Hurricane used tried and tested older technology. As a boy, Hurricane designer Sydney Camm had designed and built gliders and many model airplanes. He developed a keen eye for designs that would make good, stable aircraft.

Camm's inspiration for the Hurricane resulted from his many years designing biplanes. It was a

perfect blend of old and new, using proven concepts and materials to create a new fighter that was adapted to modern aerial warfare.

Though it used older technologies, the Hurricane was a fighter of many firsts. It was the first RAF fighter to exceed 300 miles per hour (483kmh) in level flight. It was the first to have an enclosed cockpit and retractable landing gear, and the first monoplane fighter to enter service with the RAF in combat. It was also the first RAF fighter to down a Luftwaffe bomber, a Heinkel He 111.

One of the Hurricane's intrinsic strengths came from its jointed tubular frame and wood construction. (Another RAF legend, the de Havilland Mosquito, also benefitted from this seemingly obsolete construction.) This made the Hurricane lighter than contemporary fighters, yet much more resilient to hardships of air combat. Often, enemy bullets passed through the fuselage's fabric covering without causing serious damage. Another advantage to this simple construction was that it could be repaired in workshops by men with basic mechanical skills, making it possible to fix damaged Hurricanes and return them to service quickly. Around 60 percent of Hurricanes downed in Britain were put back in service.

This British Hawker Hurricane IIA (RAF serial number Z2963), seen here in November 1941, was used for evaluation of stability and flight control at the US National Advisory Committee for Aeronautics (NACA) Langley Research Center, Virginia.

RIGHT: Hurricane Mk IICs of No. 1 Squadron fly in echelon formation near RAF Tangmere station in 1942.

FOLLOWING PAGES: **Desert Wind.** Hawker Hurricane Mk IIDs of No. 6 Squadron, armed with rockets and Vickers S 40-millimeter cannons, catch vehicles of Rommel's Afrika Korps in the open and unleash a devastating attack. These "tank buster" Hurricanes were the bane of German ground troops and armor during the North African campaign; their rugged construction and the heavy-hitting firepower of the 40-millimeter cannons made a great platform for a ground-attack aircraft. Usually, one or two well-placed rounds were enough to knock out German armor. The rockets could lay down a blanket of destruction and didn't require a direct hit to take out vehicles and troops.

Not surprisingly, then, the Hurricane was greatly admired by pilots who flew it. In his book *Duel of Eagles*, Captain Peter Townsend wrote:

> By December [1938] we had our full initial equipment of sixteen aircraft. The Fury [biplane] had been a delightful play-thing; the Hurricane was a thoroughly war-like machine, rock solid as a platform for eight Browning machine-guns, highly maneuverable despite its large proportions and with an excellent view from the cockpit. The Hurricane lacked the speed and glamour of the Spitfire and was slower than the Me 109, whose pilots were to develop contempt for it and a snobbish preference for being shot down by Spitfires. But figures were to prove that during the Battle of Britain, machine for machine, the Hurricane would acquit itself every bit as well as the Spitfire and in the aggregate (there were more than three Hurricanes to two Spitfires) do greater damage among the Luftwaffe.

I spoke with Townsend at a symposium in 1991 and asked him his opinion of the Hurricane versus the Spitfire. He indicated that both airplanes were very good, with each having its good and bad points. He thought the biggest factor, more than the aircraft, was the pilot. He saw the two airplanes more as complements to each other than competitors.

In 2010, Ben Bowring, formerly of No. 111 Squadron, told the *Daily Mail* that the Hurricane "would keep flying almost after it was destroyed." On one occasion he was able to land despite heavily damaged wings. "That aircraft's a bloody miracle," he commented afterward.

The Germans had a different opinion of the Hurricane. Although almost as many Luftwaffe fighters were shot down by Hurricanes as by Spitfires, Germans didn't like to admit they were brought down by a wood-and-fabric fighter. It was considered more of an honor to be brought down by the Spitfire.

According to David Alan Johnson, writing in the November 1994 issue of *Aviation History*:

> Die-hard defenders of the Hurricane are quick to comment that the Hawker aircraft is credited with shooting down more enemy aircraft than the Spitfire. The Air Ministry confirmed this with its statement, "The total number of enemy aircraft brought down by single-seater fighters was in the proportion of 3 by Hurricanes to 2 by Spitfires," and also noted, "the average proportion . . . of serviceable [aircraft] each morning was approximately 63 percent Hurricanes and 37 percent Spitfires." A cynic might be tempted to say that the Hurricane did most of the work, but the Spitfire got most of the glory.

It is important to remember that the Hurricane is oftentimes overshadowed by the legendary status of the Spitfire. There's no doubt the Spitfire was a terrific airplane, with its sleek and sexy lines, but it was not as robust as the Hurricane, nor did it do as much of the work, with at least 60 percent of RAF Squadrons being equipped with Hurricanes. Johnson's *Aviation History* article sums it up succinctly: "The fact that the Hurricane was responsible for more enemy aircraft destroyed is eclipsed by the Spitfire's graceful silhouette and romantic legend. Glamour usually outshines performance, in war as in love."

In his book *Hurricane: The Last Witnesses*, Brian Milton honors the Hurricane and its pilots:

> In the Battle of Britain, Hurricanes scored the highest number of RAF victories, accounting for 1,593 out of the 2,739 total claimed. By the beginning of 1941 German pilots had their measure. It did not do for a [Messerschmitt] Bf 109 to get into a dogfight with Hurricanes because the Hurricane could out-turn it, but the Bf 109 pilots' "dive and zoom" tactics put Hurricane pilots at a severe disadvantage. . . .
>
> Without the Hurricane, the Battle of Britain would have been lost. A total of 1,715 Hurricanes flew with Fighter Command during the period of the battle, far in excess of all other British fighters combined. Having entered service a year before the Spitfire, the Hurricane was "half a generation" older, and markedly inferior in terms of speed and climb. . . . Unlike the Spitfire, it was a wholly operational, go-anywhere, do-anything fighter by July 1940.

Beyond the Battle of Britain, the Hurricane served on every front throughout the war. More than 2,500 Hurricanes served in the Soviet Air Force. Hurricanes fought in the Battle of France and covered the extraction of British troops at Dunkirk. Over the deserts of North Africa, Hurricanes helped bring about Rommel's defeat. They fought over the steaming jungles of Burma against the Japanese, and they served over the cold Atlantic, defending convoys from air attacks.

In a sense, the Hurricane had two wars to fight: one against the Allies' enemies and one against the false perception of Spitfire superiority. The Hurricane doggedly drove through all adversities and, like the workhorse it was, completed every task assigned to it. It deserves all honors that can be heaped upon it, not least of which is the title of one of history's greatest fighter aircraft.

HAWKER HURRICANE

AIRCRAFT DEPICTED
Hurricane Mk I
Flown by Squadron Leader Peter Townsend
No. 85 Squadron
Croydon, Surrey, England
August 31, 1940

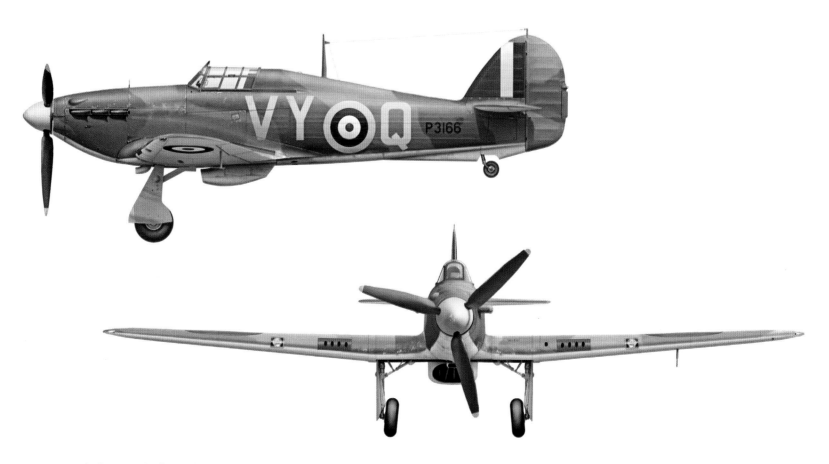

DESIGNER: Sydney Camm
MANUFACTURER: Hawker Aircraft Ltd.
AIRFRAMES PRODUCED: 14,533

SPECIFICATIONS

Length . . . . 31 ft 5 in (9.59m)	Output . . . . 1,030 hp
Wingspan . . . . 40 ft (12.19m)	Maximum speed . . . . 317 mph (510kmh)
Height . . . . 13 ft 11.5 in (4.25m)	Cruising speed. . . . . 272 mph (438kmh)
Empty weight . . . . .5,658 lb (2,566kg)	Ceiling . . . . 34,000 ft (10,363m)
Loaded weight . . . . .6,600 lb (2,994kg)	Range . . . . .529 mi (851km)
Engine . . . . .Rolls-Royce Merlin II or III	Armament . . . . Browning .303-in machine guns × 8

HAWKER HURRICANE

1. Radio contactor master switch
2. Cockpit light dimmer switch
3. Generator switch
4. Oil dilution pushbutton
5. Landing lamp control lever
6. Oxygen supply cock
7. R/T remote controller
8. Throttle control
9. Propeller speed control
10. Throttle lever friction adjuster
11. Landing lamp switch
12. Cockpit lights
13. Supercharger control
14. Fuel cock
15. Undercarriage emergency release lever
16. Rudder trim tab control
17. Elevator trim tab control
18. Radiator flap control lever
19. Hood catch control
20. Engine starter button
21. Booster coil pushbutton
22. Boost control cutout
23. Oxygen regulator
24. Clock
25. Undercarriage indicator on/off switch
26. Undercarriage indicator changeover switch
27. Undercarriage indicator
28. Reflector gunsight
29. Reflector light spare lamps
30. Tachometer
31. Reflector light switch

32. Boost gauge
33. Fuel tank selector switch
34. Fuel gauge
35. Fuel pressure warning light
36. Radiator temperature gauge
37. Oil pressure gauge
38. Gun camera switch
39. Navigation lights switch
40. Pressure head heater switch
41. Ignition switches
42. Fuel tank pressurizing control
43. Oil temperature gauge
44. Cylinder priming pump
45. Signaling switch box
46. Emergency exit panel jettison lever
47. Hydraulic hand pump
48. Flap indicator
49. Seat adjustment lever
50. Undercarriage and flap selector lever
51. Pilot's seat
52. Control column and spade grip
53. Gun firing button
54. Compass
55. Rudder pedals
56. Windscreen deicing pump
57. Air speed indicator
58. Artificial horizon
59. Rate of climb indicator
60. Altimeter
61. Direction indicator
62. Turn and bank indicator
63. Brake pressure gauge

CHAPTER 3

LOCKHEED P-38
Lightning

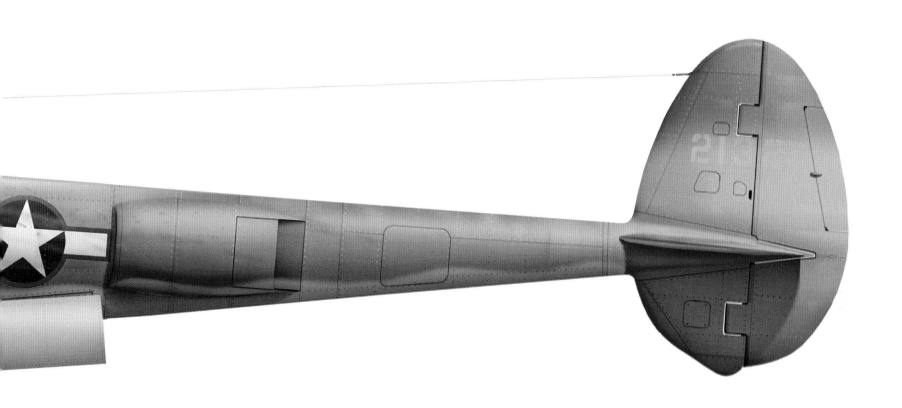

The Lockheed P-38 Lightning, the first fighter aircraft to reach 400 miles per hour (640kmh), was perhaps the most interesting single-seat fighter aircraft design of World War II. Its planform silhouette was easily recognizable virtually around the world, even in far-off places like New Guinea, where the native population called it "the twin body airplane." What might be more interesting and less known about the Lightning is its long journey to becoming one of the war's best fighters and only the American fighter aircraft to remain in production throughout the entire American involvement in World War II.

The P-38's story began in the mid-1930s, with the United States maintaining an isolationist stance, having just emerged from First World I and suffering through the Great Depression. Public sentiment was against involvement in the war that was developing in Europe, and the US government had maintained (if only publicly) that America would not participate in what was deemed to be a war not of our concern.

During the interwar period, military development seemed marked by a lack of direction, organization, and cooperation among politicians, the government, and the branches of the military. Politicians saw little need to develop new technologies and didn't want to waste what little money was available for ventures that would net no political or financial gain. The army and the navy were locked in a fierce rivalry and continually fought over the limited funds available for aircraft production contracts. On top of this, the military saw no urgent need for new technology, underestimating the rapidly evolving aircraft designs of foreign countries while overestimating the capabilities of US designs. Besides, there had been no official declaration of war, so why push new technology?

Despite this restrictive political-military climate, a new aircraft design *was* imagined, at least in the minds of two Lockheed designers: Hall Hibbard and Clarence "Kelly" Johnson. Their design was submitted in response to the requirements set forth in the newly formed category of interceptor, which was formulated to circumvent the existing fighter design rules that limited aircraft ammunition loads to 500 pounds (227kg) and engine ratings to 500 horsepower.

Hibbard and Johnson's design was called the Model 22, and it exceeded all previous design parameters and performance figures. It called for two Allison V-1710 engines of 1,150 horsepower housed in twin

Until the Last Moment. Major Tommy McGuire was the second-highest ranking US ace of World War II with thirty-eight victories (right behind Maj. Dick Bong, who had forty). On January 7, 1945, McGuire led a flight of four P-38s to the Japanese airfield at Fabrica on the island of Negros in the Philippines. McGuire's tenure was just about up, and he wanted to increase his score before he was shipped back to the United States. Over Negros, the P-38s encountered a couple of Ki-43 "Oscars," one of which was piloted by veteran ace Akira Sugimoto, who quickly downed one of the Lightnings. Sugimoto was a formidable opponent, and his nimble fighter was soon closing in on a second P-38, which was piloted by Capt. Ed Weaver. McGuire called on the radio for Weaver to drop tanks and pull hard to the left while he cut in front of the Oscar to draw its fire away. For some reason, however, McGuire didn't drop his own tanks, perhaps wrestling with the P-38 in his tight, steep-angle turn. A split second later, his plane snap-rolled to the left at low altitude and impacted the ground inverted, killing him instantly. McGuire's quest for glory was pushed aside in a heroic attempt to spare one of his pilots—loyal to his men until the last moment.

PREVIOUS PAGES: P-38G Lightning flown by 2nd Lt. Earl E. Helms, 23rd Fighter Group, 449th Fighter Squadron, August 1943.

This shot of a P-38 from Air Group 26 at Chico, California, in December 1944, offers a stunning view of Clarence "Kelly" Johnson's design.

nacelles and tail booms, with the pilot sitting in the center in a gondola-style cockpit. The engines were counterrotating to overcome left-turning tendencies.

It would carry 400 gallons (1,500L) of internal fuel and could exceed 350 knots at combat altitudes. Construction of the first prototype, called the XP-38, began in July 1938, and the first test flight took place on January 27, 1939, at March Field, California.

Army Lt. Ben Kelsey was the test pilot on the XP-38's maiden flight when the first of several design flaws were revealed. Many of these large and small problems were gradually resolved, and testing continued until February 1939, when the army asked Lieutenant Kelsey to make the first long-range flight in the sleek fighter. The destination was Mitchel Field, Long Island, and the flight was made in record-breaking time. Carburetor icing, however, caused Kelsey to make a forced landing on a golf course short of the intended airfield. The XP-38 was destroyed, but Kelsey survived with minor injuries.

Despite the crash, the new design more than impressed the army, and thirteen development aircraft were ordered, designated the YP-38, with the first of the series flying in September 1940. By this time, the Battle of Britain was raging in the skies over England, revealing many lessons about air combat at altitude and the requirements of fighter aircraft. More improvements were made to the new twin-engine fighter, and the first combat-capable version ordered by the US Army Air Forces (USAAF) was designated the P-38D. The D model was the first combat-capable variant and was fitted with self-sealing tanks, detailed aerodynamic changes, duraluminum props, a low-pressure oxygen system, and typically a 23-millimeter cannon. In an *Air Power Australia* technical report, aeronautical engineer, defense consultant, and aviation journalist Dr. Carlo Kopp notes that Lockheed delivered all thirty to the USAAF by August 1941.

Produced from September 1941 through April 1942, the P-38E saw further refinements, including a 150-round Hispano-Suiza 20-millimeter cannon and changes to the hydraulic and electrical systems, flight instruments, and nose undercarriage. In total, two thousand design changes were carried out to meet the needs of mass production.

The P-38Fs and RAF-spec nonturbocharged 322-Bs followed; 143 of the latter were ordered in April 1940 as the Lightning I. The first RAF machines were delivered for testing in March 1942. Unfortunately, the British were unhappy with the first units they received, complaining of poor high-altitude performance and

An RAF airman talks to a pilot of the USAAF's 14th Fighter Group on the wing of his P-38 at Atcham, England, in 1942. The members of the 14th Fighter Group flew their P-38s to England in midsummer that year.

In his technical report, Dr. Kopp goes on to state: The first Lightnings to see combat operations were the photo recce F-4s of the 8th Photo Group, based in Australia, flying recce sorties over New Guinea and the Coral Sea. Initial deployments of P-38D and E models saw units stationed in the Aleutians and Iceland, with the first combat kill credited to a P-38E in the Aleutians in August 1942, downing a H6K Mavis recce [reconnaissance] aircraft, soon followed by the killing of an Fw200 Condor off Iceland, by a P-38D.

As the US moved to a war footing, the P-38E was deployed during operation BOLERO to the UK together with later model P-38F aircraft. Initial deployments saw the P-38s fly the Atlantic via Greenland, led by B-17s. After some losses, subsequent aircraft were transported on ships.

The P-38Fs were fitted with 1,225-horsepower engines and had 165-gallon (625L) drop tanks at first (later 300-gallon, 1,135L), dive flaps, and improved oxygen systems. Armament now consisted of one 20-millimeter cannon and the four .50-caliber machine guns arranged in the nose. The P-38's guns were so effective they could reliably hit targets at up to 1,000 yards. Most other fighters were effective only at 100 to 250 yards.

It was in the Pacific theater that the P-38 Lightning made its mark in history by destroying more Japanese aircraft than any other Allied fighter (P-38s accounted for 1,800 kills in the Pacific theater of operations, or PTO). In fact, the United States' two leading aces of the war—Maj. Richard Bong and Maj. Thomas McGuire Jr.—flew P-38s in the PTO.

In addition to the top two US aces of World War II flying P-38s, the longest combat mission flown over water by a single-seat fighter occurred in April 1943 when sixteen P-38s from the 70th and 339th Fighter Squadrons flew 350 nautical miles (648 km) from Guadalcanal to Bougainville to intercept a flight of

compressibility in dives, among several other design shortcomings. Eventually all of these aircraft were sent back to the USAAF.

The RAF determined that many of the P-38's performance problems could have been overcome by replacing the Allison engines with Rolls-Royce Merlins, as was eventually done with the P-51 Mustang, making it one of the best fighter aircraft of the war. Lockheed did its own study of this proposal and reached the same conclusion, but the army refused to acquiesce due to pressures from US corporate interests.

When the United States entered the war in 1941, the only aircraft in its inventory that could be reasonably expected to battle Axis aircraft were the P-38D, P-30E, and P-39, none of which effectively countered the capabilities of fighters like the Messerschmitt Bf 109s and Mitsubishi Zero. These three US aircraft were utilized in all theaters in the early part of World War II with limited success.

LEFT: USAAF ace Capt. Robert L. Faurot, who served with the 39th Fighter Squadron, 35th Fighter Group, is seen with his P-38F at Schwimmer Air Base, New Guinea, in January 1943, shortly after his second kill. Faurot was shot down by Japanese A6M Zeros during the Battle of the Bismarck Sea on March 3, 1943.

Japanese fighters and bombers. One of the bombers carried Adm. Isoroku Yamamoto, commander of the Imperial Japanese Navy and architect of the Pearl Harbor attack. Yamamoto was killed, and several Japanese planes were shot down. Missions like this were made possible by the P-38's long-range capabilities and by training pilots to manage fuel and power settings.

Many typical P-38 missions would have been impossible with any other fighter. Its range and payload made it the clear aircraft of choice in various mission profiles. The P-38 also performed well in the Mediterranean theater, for example, as a long-range escort, in fighter sweeps, and in ground and shipping attacks.

In the European theater, it was a different story. The P-47 Thunderbolt had already been chosen as the escort fighter for Allied bombers to Germany, achieving operational status with the 4th Fighter Group in early 1943. It came with fewer problems than the P-38 at that time, and although its gas-guzzling radial engine limited its operating range, it was reliable. By fall 1943, P-38s were being used alongside P-47s, but the earlier P-38 variants were still experiencing numerous problems. Pilots complained of poor oxygen systems and almost no cabin heat, resulting in a number of cases of frostbitten hands and feet. The canopy glass would frost up, and the superchargers and intercoolers

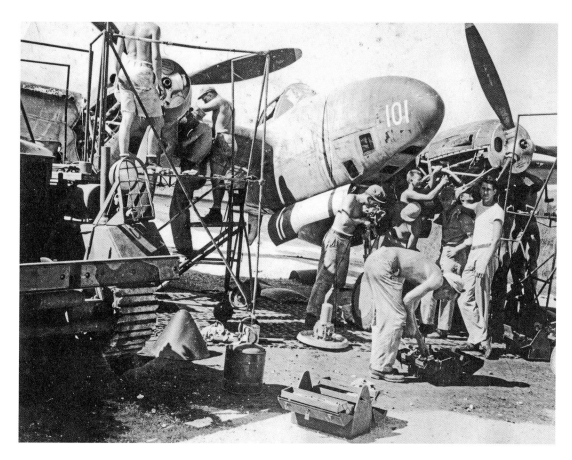

No fewer than ten ground crewmembers work to get a P-38 of the 14th Photo Recon Squadron back in the air.

most P-38s and P-47s were being assigned to ground support and other roles by spring 1944.

Lockheed was not deterred and worked endlessly until it had addressed all of the P-38's deficiencies, achieving great success with the P-38J-25 and culminating with the P-38L-0 series. The P-38 was a complicated aircraft, and pilots of the pre–J and L models faced complex tasks that required constant hands-on attention. With the L variant, Lockheed had made many of the hands-on systems function automatically, thus greatly diminishing task overload and letting pilots focus more on fighting the enemy.

Almost three thousand P-38Js and four thousand P-38Ls were built by the end of the war. These models best exemplified the type and were used in every combat role, including photo reconnaissance (F4 and F5), bomber (Droop Snoot), and pathfinder (Js and Ls equipped with AN/APS-15 navigation/attack radar). The P-38M (Piggy Back) and the P-38M-L0 were equipped with AN/APS-4 air-intercept radar for night fighting.

By war's end, 10,037 P-38 Lightnings had been built across all variants. These aircraft operated in every theater, including Alaska and the Aleutian Islands, and served in every USAAF combat group. During the postwar years, P-38s were flown by the Free French Air Forces (Group 2/33) and the Italian Air Force (3rd Aerobrigata RT and 4th Aerobrigata).

★ ★ ★

caused lead additives to separate from the fuel, resulting in detonations and engine failures. At altitude, the oil coolers would cause the oil to congeal.

Back in the United States, the P-51 Mustang was looking like the best prospect for the job of long-range bomber escort, focusing production and design efforts on that aircraft, which soon became the darling of the USAAF. It was a much cheaper aircraft to build, easier to fly, and much less complicated than the P-38. Gradually, all US fighter units were replacing their P-47s and P-38s with P-51s. P-38s were still used as bomber escorts, especially during 1943 and extending into the summer of 1944, by which time P-51s were present in sufficient numbers to take over the escort role. Even with several factors stacking the odds against the P-38, it achieved tremendous success against Axis fighters. Nonetheless,

The outwardly slender and graceful appearance of the P-38 Lightning belies the many complexities hidden beneath its aluminum skin. Beauty is only skin deep, as the saying goes. Yet, to see one fly and hear the low roar of its two V-12 Allison engines pull it effortlessly through the sky, it's hard to imagine this aircraft ever had any flaws.

The history of the P-38 is a combination of stunning success and disappointment. In the Pacific theater, it destroyed more enemy aircraft than all other types combined. America's two top aces, in any theater,

ABOVE: A P-38 of the 8th Photo Recon Group lines up on the runway at Saipan.

LEFT: **_Fighter Two—Guadalcanal._** Fighter Two air strip, located in the inhospitable coastal jungle of Guadalcanal, was home to one of the war's most famous P-38 units during World War II: the 339th Fighter Squadron. On April 18, 1943, the 339th took off on a special mission called Operation Vengeance, designed to assassinate Japanese Imperial Navy Commander Adm. Isoroku Yamamoto, the architect of the Pearl Harbor attack.

The Americans had deciphered Japanese military communication codes and learned that Yamamoto would be flying to Bougainville Island on an inspection tour. The Japanese adhered very strictly to schedules, and US intelligence learned Yamamoto's flight would leave Rabaul at precisely 0600. The US command was able to plan the long flight to intercept Yamamoto.

The 339th flew an unprecedented 420-mile flight 50 feet above the water toward Bougainville. As they approached the island, they saw a flight of three "Betty" bombers and a number of Zero fighters over the coast; the P-38s split up, one section attacking the fighters and one section going after the bombers. As P-38 pilot Rex Barber neared one of the bombers, he fired a burst into its right wing and engine, sending it down into the jungle and killing Yamamoto. The Japanese had lost one of their most important commanders—a blow from which they would never recover.

Richard Bong (forty victories) and Thomas McGuire Jr. (thirty-eight victories), flew P-38s in the Pacific theater. But the early variants presented some difficulties for their pilots. Cockpit management was cumbersome, and engines were prone to failure in certain conditions, forcing pilots to abort and return to their airfield. Poor cockpit heat and frosted canopy glass added to the exasperation.

The forward-thinking design and boundary-busting technology of the P-38 made it a test bed for many new innovations. Not surprisingly, its advanced design and complex internal systems required a more protracted developmental period than contemporary aircraft of this era. It had the look of a winner from the start, but, like a wild mustang lassoed in the open grasslands, it required patience and perseverance to elicit its best performance. That was the character of the P-38 from its inception, and its combat record would eventually become as striking as its appearance.

Testimony from pilots who flew the P-38, and opinions of those who fought against it, might help separate the reality from the myth. Jeffrey Ethell was a pilot, historian, and author who spent a great deal of time investigating the Lightning and writing about it. His father, Ervin Ethell, flew the P-38 in combat in World War II, and Jeff grew up listening to his father's stories. Jeff logged some hours flying a P-38L himself, and he shared his insights in books, interviews, and magazine articles. In *The Great Book of World War II Airplanes*, which Ethell coauthored, Luftwaffe pilots recounted their experiences fighting the P-38.

In his book *P-38 Lightning*, Ethell wrote:

Oberleutnant Franz Steigler, a 28 victory ace in the Bf 109 with JG 27 in North Africa, said the P-38s "could turn inside us with ease and they could go from level flight to climb almost instantaneously. We lost quite a few pilots who tried to make an attack and then pull up. The P-38s were on them at once. They closed so quickly that there was little one could do except roll quickly and dive down, for while the P-38 could turn inside us, it rolled very slowly through the first 5 or 10 degrees of bank, and by then we would already be gone. One cardinal rule we never forgot was: avoid fighting a P-38 head on. That was suicide. Their armament was so heavy and their firepower so murderous, that no one ever tried that type of attack more than once.

Johannes Steinhoff, Kommodore of Jagdgeschwader (JG) 77 in North Africa, Sicily, and Italy, and a Bf 109 pilot, concurred with Steigler, later writing in *Messerschmitts over Sicily*, "I had encountered the long-range P-38 Lightning fighter during the last few days of the North African campaign. Our opinion of this twin-boomed, twin-engined aircraft was divided. Our old Messerschmitts were still, perhaps, a little faster. But pilots who had fought them said that the Lightnings were capable of appreciably tighter turns and that they would

be on your tail before you knew what was happening. The machine guns mounted on the nose supposedly produced a concentration of fire from which there was no escape. Certainly the effect was reminiscent of a watering can when one of these dangerous apparitions started firing tracer, and it was essential to prevent them maneuvering into a position from which they could bring their guns to bear."

Luftwaffe ace Heinz Knoke, who flew the Bf 109 with JG 1 and JG 11, wrote of his encounters with the P-38 in his book *I Flew for the Führer*, "It flies like the devil himself, turning, diving, and climbing almost like a rocket. I am never able to fire more than a few pot-shots."

A P-38H of the Army Air Forces Tactical Center in Orlando, Florida, carries two 1,000-pound bombs during capability tests in March 1944. The tests were conducted to determine the feasibility of using the P-38 for fighter-bomber missions against Germany and Japan.

After flying the P-38, Jeffrey Ethell wrote an article for *Flight* giving his impressions of the aircraft including preflight, takeoff, maneuvers, and landing. "After a few tentative turns, with absolutely no pressure from the ailerons," he observed, "I was beginning to comprehend why everyone loved the Lightning so much: it flies like a jet with no vibration and light controls. . . . The single dominant impression is this thing is smooth and effortless to fly—quite unlike the more complex warbird types."

Ethell's comments seem to contradict some of what has been written about this fighter, but remember he flew the P-38L, the series that had resolved all the issues of the earlier models and realized the full potential of this thoroughbred fighter design.

Ethell wrote more about the P-38's other virtues. The wheel and yoke steering system, he noted, gave complete and balanced control of the aircraft, with a light feel and very good response to control inputs; the ergonomically natural position of the pilot's arms when holding the control wheel reduced fatigue on flights of long duration; by using a combination of control inputs and uneven power settings on either engine, it was possible to execute maneuvers that could not be matched by other fighters; the stall characteristics were docile, and the earlier problems with compressibility in dives were gone due to dive slats under the P-38L's wings.

Ethell summed up his flight experience by writing, "Reining back some obvious prejudice from growing up with Dad's memories, I have come to see the P-38 in a far different light. There is little doubt in my mind I have flown the finest American fighter of WWII. It may have taken a little more time to master and certainly was more complex to maintain in the field, but the options available to the Lightning pilot were impressive. A talented, aggressive fighter pilot could clearly make the P-38 sing."

The 475th Fighter Group became one of the most successful units with the P-38. One of its pilots, Carroll "Andy" Anderson, flew the P-38 in the group's "Satan's Angels" squadron, and he wrote an article in the May 1988 issue of *Airpower* that, in the editor's words, "established an authenticated body of information about this famous, but often misunderstood aircraft."

Anderson's piece is a reliable account of fighting in the P-38 based on his experiences flying against the Japanese:

> As long as the P-38 pilot kept alert, entered combat at high speed and then pulled away to resume the contest on terms of his own choosing, he was difficult to bring down. His aircraft's unusually long endurance, up to 2,600 miles [4,185 km] with tanks, allowed him time to make repeated passes, and its firepower of one 20mm cannon and four .50 caliber machine guns, all of it mounted in the nose, put out a lethal amount of high velocity shells. The only way a P-38 pilot could be defeated— and it happened all too frequently—was if he disregarded the warning never to dogfight with opponents, thereby ending up in a turning contest, which lost him speed and altitude.

Rough field operations caused difficult working conditions for 9th Air Force maintenance personnel. Here, a crew prepares an external heater to warm a P-38's frozen engine as an armorer works on the nose guns while standing atop a makeshift stand.

The P-38 performed better on the vertical plane, climbing or diving very quickly, but was slower in turning, making it not so effective in a horizontal fight. Pilots were advised not to become involved in a turning fight with the lighter, more maneuverable Japanese aircraft. Also, downward visibility was impaired by the wings and two large engines on either side, making banking left or right necessary to see below. The P-38's cockpit was comfortable and, unlike in Europe, the heating system was not an issue for pilots in the Pacific, since most of their missions were at lower altitudes. In fact, the cockpit was usually quite hot, but if the side windows were rolled down in flight severe buffeting would develop on the tail plane. As a result, some pilots flew in shorts, T-shirts, and tennis shoes.

ABOVE: Major Richard Bong served with the 49th Fighter Group in Darwin, Australia, and Port Moresby, New Guinea. He scored forty kills over Japanese aircraft en route to becoming the top US ace of World War II.

OPPOSITE: *Scat Attack.* Lieutenant Robin Olds, flying his new P-38J *Scat II*, leads the 434th Squadron of the 479th Fighter Group on a strafing run on the German-controlled airfield of Nancy-Essey, France, on August 18, 1944. Post-mission evaluation would conclude that thirty-two P-38s had destroyed forty-three German aircraft and damaged twenty-three more. Three day later, Olds became an ace.

"In spite of the awesome array of gauges and dials in the cockpit of the Lockheed P-38, the basic instruments were easily located," Anderson went on to write. "Further, the various handles, knobs, and gadgets required for landing gear, flaps, etc., came easily to hand, although post war criticism of the Lightning cockpit has run the gamut from condemnation of the fuel cross feed system to cockpit heating, and to the fact that the flap handle was located on the right side of the cockpit requiring a deal of ambidexterity alien to some fighter pilots."

It is important to note that in the skies over Europe, the P-38 was the United States' main long-range fighter until the P-51 entered the war. In fact, The P-38 flew more 130,000 sorties in the European theater. The P-38 had protected bomber streams to and from Germany during the most critical months of 1943 and 1944. In this role, the P-38s operated at higher altitudes to cover the bombers, which is where fuel and oil problems developed in early models. Many pilots had to abort due to engine problems, and the P-38 gained a reputation among bomber crews. That stigma remained even after the J and L models entered operation.

One of my father's friends, Wendell, a top turret gunner on a B-17 bomber, told me about a mission during which his opinion about the P-38 was changed completely. It was an "all out" run to Germany in the winter of 1944. Every single bomber available had to be used, and he was assigned to a war-weary B-17 they called a "hangar queen."

Once airborne, the B-17's crew discovered that the electrical outlets for their heated flight suits were not functional, forcing them to fly the entire mission in the bitter cold. At 28,000 feet (8,535m) the thermometer recorded an outside temperature of -78 degrees Fahrenheit. Sitting in his turret behind the pilots, Wendell spotted a single Fw 190 boring in on them from four o'clock. Suddenly, the Focke-Wulf pulled

into a vertical climb. A second later he saw a P-38 in a vertical climb on the German's tail. He watched as both planes continued to climb vertically until he could barely see them. Shortly afterward, the German plane spiraled down on fire with the P-38 trailing it for a brief time. He then noticed a tiny white parachute and realized the German pilot had managed to bail out. Having heard many rumors about the P-38's inabilities at high altitude, Wendell was so amazed that for a few seconds he forgot about his painful, useless hands. Supposedly a P-38 was incapable of fighting at high altitude, yet he and his crew had just been saved by one of these twin-tailed fighters. Afterward, Wendell spent several months in the hospital, almost losing his hands to frostbite and wondering who the P-38 pilot was who had saved his life.

As the Fw 190 pilot discovered, trying to evade a P-38 by climbing or diving usually cost you the fight, and possibly your life. The enemy's best chance against a P-38 on his tail was to roll away quickly.

All experienced fighter pilots learned the strengths and weaknesses of their fighters, as well as those of their opponents', both of which they exploited to their advantage.

In 1939, one of the first P-38 prototype aircraft set a speed record from California to New York in 7 hours and 2 minutes, but it crashed short of its intended airport due to carburetor icing.

In total, more than ten thousand P-38s were produced during World War II, making it one of the most successful fighters and interceptors of its time despite being very unlike other fighter designs of its time. Like other new aircraft designs, its life began with a testing period to iron out the ripples and flaws—although its test period ran on a bit longer to make it nearly perfect—and to many, quite possibly the greatest piston-powered fighter in history.

LOCKHEED P-38
Lightning

AIRCRAFT DEPICTED

P-38J-15-LO Lightning, S/N 42-103993, *Marge*
Flown by Captain Richard Bong
9th Fighter Squadron, 49th Fighter Group
August 1943

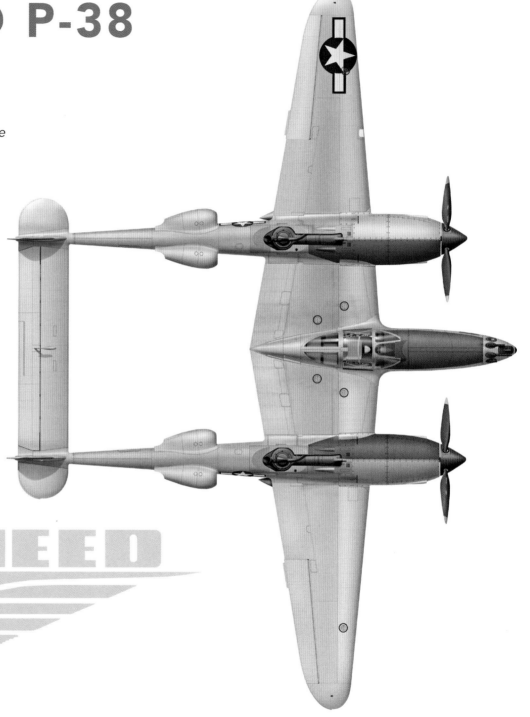

DESIGNER: Clarence "Kelly" Johnson
MANUFACTURER: Lockheed Corporation
AIRFRAMES PRODUCED: 10,037

SPECIFICATIONS

Length . . . . .37 ft 10 in (11.53m)	Maximum speed . . . . 414 mph (666kmh)
Wingspan. . . . . 52 ft (15.85m)	Cruising speed. . . . . 275 mph (443kmh)
Height . . . . .12 ft 10 in (3.91m)	Landing speed. . . . . 85 mph (137kmh)
Empty weight. . . . . .12,780 lb (5,797kg)	Ceiling . . . . 44,000 ft (13,400m)
Loaded weight. . . . . .17,500 lb (7,938kg)	Range . . . . 972 mi (1,565km)
Engines . . . Allison V-1710-89/91 liquid-cooled V-12 × 2	Armament . . . . .20mm cannon × 1
Output. . . . . .1,425 hp × 2	.50-caliber machine guns × 4

LOCKHEED P-38
Lightning

1. L-3 optical reflector gunsight
2. Hatch release handle
3. Hatch release buttons
4. Hatch locking arm
5. Cockpit light
6. Nose-gun compartment heat control
7. 5-inch (27mm) rockets fusebox
8. Standby magnetic compass
9. Suction gauge
10. Clock
11. Compass indicator
12. Directional gyro
13. Gyro horizon
14. Dual-manifold pressure gauge
15. Dual tachometer
16. Mixture controls
17. Coolant shutter controls
18. Throttle levers
19. Reserve fuel tank gauge
20. Altimeter
21. Airspeed indicator
22. Turn and bank indicator
23. Rate of climb indicator
24. Port engine oil temp, oil pressure, and fuel pressure gauge
25. Coolant temperature gauge
26. Carburetor air temperature gauge
27. Circuit breakers
28. Flap control lever

29. Radio off pushbutton and frequency selector pushbuttons
30. Recognition light switches
31. Elevator tab control
32. Bomb- or tank-release selector switch
33. Oxygen pressure gauge
34. Rudder pedals
35. Propeller feathering switch warning light
36. Oxygen flow indicator
37. Oxygen regulator
38. Parking brake handle
39. Dive recovery flap control switch
40. Control wheel
41. Control column
42. Aileron boost shutoff valve
43. Window crank handles
44. Landing gear control handle
45. Detrola receiver tuning knob
46. Cockpit ventilator control
47. Starboard and port tank selector valves
48. Outer wing tank low-level check button and auxiliary fuel pump switches
49. Seat adjustment lever
50. Pilot's seat
51. Machine gun button (left) and cannon button (right)
52. Cockpit heat control
53. Propeller controls
54. Propeller selector switches
55. Microphone switch

MITSUBISHI
A6M Zero

CHAPTER **4**

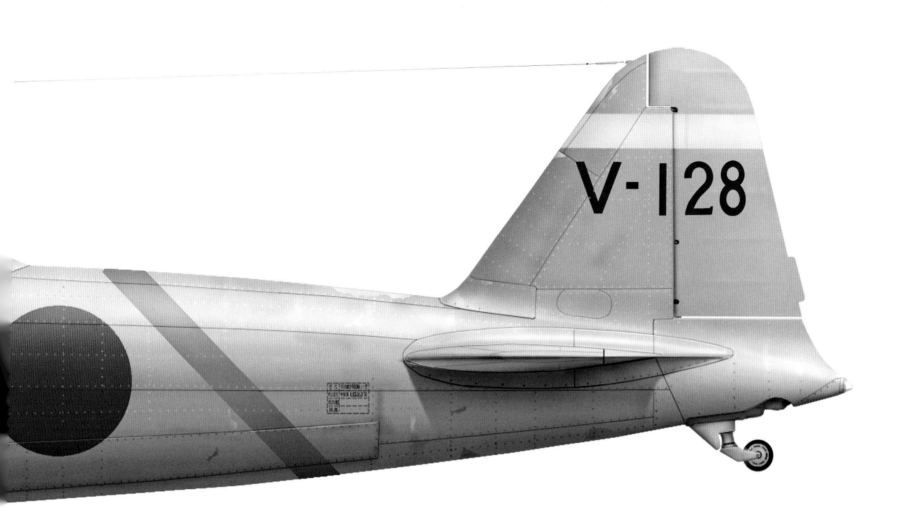

K nown in Japan as the Rei-shiki Kanjō Sentōki (abbreviated Rei-sen), the Mitsubishi A6M quickly made its presence known around the world, gaining a fearsome and almost mystical reputation as the Japanese Zero, so named for its carrier fighter designation, Type 0.

Contrary to what some believe, the Zero was not created as a fighter to be deployed against America, but was a request by the Imperial Japanese Navy for a superior fighter to deploy against China when the Second Sino-Japanese War began in 1937. Recognizing that other nations were developing advanced aircraft, Japan's navy wanted a carrier-based fighter with long-range capabilities that would not only help support military operations inside China but rival all other emerging aircraft designs.

In the 1920s, Japan solicited the help of Great Britain in flight training, tactics, and engineering, resulting in several new navy fighter aircraft, many of them biplanes. Still, these early aircraft were superior to anything the Chinese could put up in opposition.

The Imperial Japanese Navy sought a more sophisticated fighter to compete with rapidly advancing aviation technology, so a request was issued to two Japanese companies for a modern monoplane fighter design of all-metal construction. The two companies, Nakajima and Mitsubishi, accepted the challenge. It was clear to the engineers that the military wanted an aircraft that was the best in the world—a tall order for any Japanese aviation firm at the time.

At Mitsubishi, the task fell to the head of design, Jirō Horikoshi. A graduate of the Facility of Aeronautics in Tokyo, Horikoshi had spent time in Europe and America studying aircraft design and manufacturing. The new fighter design was originally designated the 12-shi (shi being an abbreviation meaning "trial manufacture" or "experimental").

One of the biggest problems the team faced was the quality of the available engines. The design brief specified a very light but powerful fighter, but the Japanese aviation industry in the 1930s was just out of its embryonic stage, and much of its technology was somewhat unreliable and untested. The military's requested specifications, combined with the state of the industry, made for a difficult environment in which to work for a forward-thinking designer like Horikoshi. Most of the engines being produced there were either too heavy or lacked the power to satisfy both requirements. The engine eventually chosen (starting with the third prototype) was the 950-horsepower Sakae 12, a fourteen-cylinder, air-cooled, twin-row radial developed by Nakajima. The first two A6M1 airframes had carried the 875-horsepower Mitsubishi Zuisei 13, which was abandoned when the Sakae 12 proved superior. It is interesting to note that the Sakae had some internal components of Pratt & Whitney origin, Japan having previously secured a license to manufacture some these parts.

Hickam Field—Second Attack. Mitsubishi Zeros from the aircraft carrier *Akagi* fly top cover as BN5 Kates from the carrier *Zuikaku* drop 250-kilogram (550-pound) bombs on the hangars and runways at Hickam Field during the second attack on Pearl Harbor, December 7, 1941.

PREVIOUS PAGES: A6M2 Model 21 Zero flown by Pilot Officer 1st Class Saburō Sakai, August 1942.

Further exasperation came when disagreement arose among expert military advisors as to what the Zero fighter should be. One side thought speed and heavier firepower was imperative, another wanted a lighter, more maneuverable fighter. Disagreements stalled development and almost caused the cancellation of the project. Fortunately everyone eventually agreed that the success of the new fighter in combat would ultimately depend mostly on pilot skill, and progress should be resumed without further delay. Horikoshi had a lot to consider in ensuring the promised success of the Zero, but he accepted the burden of his responsibility in stride.

Horikoshi reported to the Japanese navy that all the requirements could be met with his new fighter as long as the design was kept light in construction and very simple. This meant no accessories, no pilot armor, no heavy armament, and no fuel tank protection. Even the weight of a parachute pack was taken into consideration—pilots were advised they could use them at their discretion, which suggested to them that no parachute would make their airplane lighter and therefore a more effective weapon. Dispensing with these features, which were found on fighter aircraft of other nations, was not just a matter of necessity. It was also a reflection of the samurai code of Bushido, in which the courage and skill of the Japanese warrior was more important than the weapon itself. The increased danger from a lack of safety equipment was acceptable to most Japanese pilots as a matter of honor, pride, and courage.

On March 23, 1939, the first Zero made its maiden flight. In 1940, testing of the new Zero fighter A6M1 was completed with every requirement met except top speed. Armament consisted of two nose-mounted 7.7-millimeter machine guns and two wing-mounted 20-millimeter cannons. The navy assigned fifteen of these preproduction aircraft to combat trials in China. Near the end of July 1940, formal production began on the Navy Type 0 carrier fighter A6M2 Model 11. By September, modifications

A war-weary and badly weathered A6M5 is rolled into a hangar.

included folding wingtips and a reinforced rear wing spar for carrier operations. With these modifications came the new designation, A6M2 Model 21—which made its American debut at Pearl Harbor on December 7, 1941.

The next Zero variant was the A6M3 Model 21, which became available in 1942. It was powered by the newer Sakae 21 engine with one- and two-stage superchargers. This engine yielded 1,130 horsepower, which only increased top speed by 5.5 knots. Pilots suggested removing the folding wingtips; the modification shortened the wingspan and gave the wingtips a squared-off appearance. The Allied codename for this model was the Zeke 32 or "Hamp."

Somewhere during production of the Model 21, the longer wingspan was reinstated with a few other modifications that led to the next major variant, the A6M5 Model 52, which had a small number of subtype modifications, mostly subtle changes to aileron size and shape, flap size, fuel capacity, and wingspan. The most recognizable modification was the introduction of several individual exhaust stacks protruding from under the cowl flaps on either side of the engine. These allowed the exhaust gases to be pushed back, which was thought to increase forward thrust. Changes to the Model 52 netted an increase of up to 13 knots in speed. During the latter part of production, the Model 52 had armored glass installed in the windscreen, and the nose guns were upsized to 13-millimeters, while the wing cannons were changed to belt-fed Oerlikon Type 99 Mk 2 models instead of the previous drum-fed cannons. The A6M5c had an unusual gun array: two Type 3 13-millimeter guns added in the wing outboard of the 20-millimeter cannons, and two nose guns, one 13-millimeter and one 7.7-millimeter. Further offensive provisions made in the A6M5c allowed it to carry air-to-air rockets under the wings. By this time, the loss of many veteran pilots finally brought about measures to preserve the lives of trained pilots. Armor plate was installed behind the pilot's seat along with a self-sealing fuel tank, and several panels of bulletproof glass were

added behind the pilot's head. Offensive provisions made in the A6M5c allowed it to carry air-to-air rockets under the wings.

The next significant Zero, the A6M7 Model 63, came with a water-methanol-injected Sakae 31 engine that could produce more power in an emergency. Intended for fighter-bomber operations, the Model 63 could carry one centerline 550-pound bomb and two underwing fuel tanks.

The last Zero fighter was to be the A6M8 with a Mitsubishi Kinsei 62 engine producing 1,350 horsepower. Two examples were built and flight-tested with positive results. An order was placed for 6,300 of the type, but none were completed by war's end.

One more significant type to mention was the floatplane version called the A6M2-N (Allied codename "Rufe"). This was an A6M2 modified for maritime operations by the addition of a single-float pontoon under the fuselage and two smaller outrigger floats under

An A6M2 Zero begins its takeoff roll on the Imperial Japanese Navy carrier *Zuikaku*.

the wings. Rufes were put into service in mid-1942 and served in many combat theaters, primarily as defensive fighters and as escorts for reconnaissance aircraft.

The Japanese military had plans to build more Zero aircraft through 1946, but the end finally came in August 1945 when the United States dropped two atomic bombs on Japan. By then, the tally of total A6M airframes built was 10,939.

★ ★ ★

I've spent a lot of my life studying aircraft, especially those of the 1930s and 1940s when piston-powered flight reached its pinnacle. So many different and brilliant designs came from that period that it is difficult to pick one that was the best overall. But if it were a contest based on beauty alone, I would have to cast my vote for the Mitsubishi A6M5 Zero. To me it was the most pleasing and perfectly balanced piston-powered aeronautical form ever created. What the Spitfire and Mustang represented aesthetically to V-12-powered aircraft, the Zero was to the radial-engine machines.

The genius of Jirō Horikoshi can only be fully appreciated when one understands the environment in which he worked and the unusual obstacles he had to overcome to create such a legendary airplane.

Japan in the 1930s had only recently emerged from a feudal and somewhat medieval past that had endured for centuries. Its transition to a modern, industrialized society had not yet fully matured, and an imbalance between old and new traditions permeated Japanese society. Nowhere was this more evident than in its government and military.

Japanese society had a centuries-old tradition of minimalism. The average citizen was conditioned to doing as much as possible with as little as possible. This cultural philosophy was best exemplified by the samurai. The basic meaning of

the term is "one who serves," and it was a title reserved for a warrior class who served nobility. Their lifestyle, though extremely disciplined and simplistic, was one dedicated to the study of a variety of subjects: art, poetry, calligraphy, philosophy, gardening, weaponry, and the art of warfare. All things were given equal attention, and each discipline was considered important to becoming well-balanced, a quality reflected in the design of the Mitsubishi Zero.

As Japan wrestled with issues related to its entrance into the modern world, the nation lagged behind others that had long before embraced modern industry. Great Britain, Germany, and the United States encouraged free thinking and free enterprise and had made greater advancements in technology than Japan by the early twentieth century.

The Japanese military still relished the old samurai code and was reluctant to break from its proud but outdated traditions. Japanese people were expected to adhere to old doctrines. When aircraft design firms were asked to create new fighters and bombers, they were

OPPOSITE: **Tiger Strikes Twice.** A Nakajima B5N2 "Kate" torpedo bomber from the Imperial Japanese Navy carrier *Shōkaku* joins up with two Mitsubishi Zeros from the carrier *Akagi* after attacking Hickam Field and targets around Pearl Harbor for a second time on December 7, 1941. Ewa Plantation and Ewa Field air base are just out of frame to the left.

BELOW: Aircraft are prepared for a morning sortie on the Imperial Japanese Navy aircraft carrier *Zuikaku*, east of the Solomon Islands, on May 5, 1942. On May 7 and 8, the carrier engaged with US Navy carriers and aircraft during the Battle of the Coral Sea.

©Jim Laurier

ABOVE: Ensign Saburō Sakai was Japan's leading ace to survive World War II.

ABOVE LEFT: These Navy Type 0 A6M3s were photographed circa 1943. The Zero got its name from this naval variant of the A6M, not from the distinct Japanese roundel, as many people erroneously believe.

expected to create the best with whatever resources were available, even if those resources were not wholly adequate. The old adage applied here: "If the only tool you have is a hammer, then every problem becomes a nail."

Jirō Horikoshi had to try to satisfy the somewhat backward-looking military powers by using technology and components that were not up to par with those of his foreign competitors. The specifications for a new fighter plane issued by the military were almost completely unachievable with materials then available. More powerful and reliable aircraft engines were needed. Further, many materials that were available were not of the best quality or were not in sufficient supply due to slow production rates and other problems. The Japanese military, however, was not concerned with these issues, nor did it want to hear any complaints. It demanded optimum results in a short period.

There were a lot of disappointments in the early stages of the Zero's creation, but Horikoshi knew exactly how to make the airplane the Imperial Navy wanted. Initially, he would have to achieve his goal with less engine than it needed, so he was forced to design his fighter to be as light as possible to optimize the power-to-weight ratio. This meant the Zero would not be a very sturdy airplane, though it would be more maneuverable than its opponents, possess speed, and have long-range capability.

The basic A6M Zero design, as we now know, was not the fastest fighter of the war. It was not the strongest, nor was it able to dive very fast due to structural weaknesses. It could not turn quickly at high speeds due to excessive forces on control surfaces. But no aircraft is perfect. Each has strengths and weaknesses. Indeed, all the types in this book filled a specific need at a specific time. Each one had a measurable effect on events in World War II, including the Mitsubishi Zero.

The Zero, like any fighter plane, was just a static machine until a human being climbed in to operate it. The effectiveness of any aircraft in performing particular tasks is largely dependent on two things: the capability of the aircraft and the pilot's ability to capitalize on its strengths while avoiding its weaknesses. When the correct balance of these considerations is achieved, the man and aircraft become one. And that is a very effective, and in the case of the Zero, deadly combination.

Early in the war, the A6M Zero operated with relative impunity, prevailing even when greatly outnumbered, albeit against early American and British types that were inferior to the Zero in some ways.

Warriors of Kaneohe. Ordnance Chief John Finn mans a .50-caliber machine gun on an open tarmac and helped defend the US Navy seaplane base at Kaneohe Bay on December 7, 1941. Though he received twenty-one wounds from shrapnel and machine-gun fire from the attacking Japanese planes, Finn maintained his position while sailors assisted him by bringing boxes of ammunition. He is credited with downing at least one aircraft, a Zero flown by Lt. Fusata Iida. Iida attempted to deliberately crash his aircraft into a hangar, barely missing it and crashing a short distance behind.

As the war progressed, the Zero and its pilots faced increasing numbers of better fighters, and although Japan's losses steadily increased, the Zero very often bested its superior opponents. Many vaunted aircraft, all considered superior, fell to Zeros: Hurricanes, Spitfires, Mustangs, P-47s, P-40s, P-38s. Not to mention the many heavily defended bombers it brought down—further evidence of skilled pilots and effective fighter planes equaling a deadly combination.

Mounting A6M losses were proportionate to a variety of factors. The loss of well-trained and experienced pilots, superior enemy tactics and aircraft, and less reliable components diminished the Zero's reign. Allied bombing depleted resources and slowed production, while poor workmanship resulting from the use of forced labor also contributed to the demise of Japan's most notorious fighter. In fact, many factors in the Zero's decline paralleled those that brought about the end of the Luftwaffe. And as with Germany's Bf 109, the Zero not only fought before and throughout the war, its production was scheduled to continue in significant numbers beyond 1945. That is a rare distinction that can't be claimed by other fighter aircraft.

Opinion is almost unanimous that the A6M flew as nicely as it looked. The cockpit was roomy, and the instruments and controls were laid out simply and

RIGHT: A Japanese Mitsubishi A6M2 at Langley Research Center, Virginia, in March 1943. On June 4, 1942, Petty Officer Tadyaoshi Koga crash-landed this aircraft on Akutan Island after an attack on Dutch Harbor, Alaska. The Zero was shipped to Langley, where it was repaired and tested. The first Zero acquired by the United States, it yielded valuable information.

OPPOSITE: *Light as a Feather*. In October 1944, the desperate Japanese unleashed the first of several suicide attacks on US ships moving ever closer to the Japanese main islands. Planes were filled with just enough fuel to reach their targets. As the pilots dived on target, they fired all their guns and either released their bombs or left them attached to detonate on impact.

Contrary to popular belief, few were eager to volunteer for these missions. Many were shamed into the missions or were "volunteered" by superiors who told them if they refused they would bring dishonor to their families and be imprisoned. After a cup of ceremonial saki laced with methamphetamine, the pilot climbed into his aircraft and was sent on his way by comrades who waved flags and hats, yelling "Banzai!"

Many of these pilots, in an old samurai tradition, wrote a death poem on paper or a silk scarf. These were meant to be presented to their families, who considered a son's death for the emperor to be a great honor. One such poem read, "Duty is heavier than a mountain / Death comes light as a feather."

LMAL 32130

logically, not unlike many of the Allied types, but perhaps with a few less instruments. (Japanese pilots had the option to add or delete certain instruments according to their preferences.) The Zero's light weight gave it a short takeoff run and short rollout when landing. It also allowed the Zero to outclimb any fighter in its class.

Writer C. Peter Chen, founder of the World War II Database website, wrote, "Most Japanese Navy pilots immediately found A6M Zero fighters to be the most efficient aircraft they had ever flown."

Saburō Sakai, one of Japan's most famous fighter aces, recalled in his book *Samurai*, cowritten with Martin Caidin, "The Zero excited me as nothing else had ever done. Even on the ground it had the cleanest lines I had ever seen in an aeroplane. It was a dream to fly."

In fact, many Allied pilots admired the Zero's design and were surprised by its aerobatic abilities. A number of Zeros fell into the hands of the Allies, and some were test flown and evaluated by US pilots. One account in the National Naval Aviation Museum archives reads, "One naval aviator and nine manufacturer test pilots logged

hops in the aircraft during the conference, giving it high marks in its ground handling, take offs, and approach and landing characteristics. When it came to combat qualities, pilots that flew the Zero concluded that the Japanese fighter was a 'dangerous airplane to dogfight at slow speeds,' stating it was 'excellent for low altitude offensive combat or any turning flight where radius of turn or maneuverability is required as prime.'"

Despite its shortcomings, the A6M Zero was a triumph in aeronautical engineering. It endures today as a modern symbol of the samurai code of excellence and purity of intent. Quoted in Robert C. Mikesh's book *Zero: Combat and Development History of Japan's Legendary Mitsubishi A6M Zero Fighter*, the airplane's designer, Jirō Horikoshi, summed up the essence of his creation: "I can claim, however, in the study of the Zero, and its ancestors and descendants, that it was original in the same degree as other planes are, and that while it contains certain special features that were all its own, it serves as a prime example of a special design created to suit an unusual set of circumstances."

MITSUBISHI
A6M Zero

AIRCRAFT DEPICTED

A6M5 Zero
Flown by Ensign Saburō Sakai
343 Kōkūtai Yokosuka Air Wing
1945

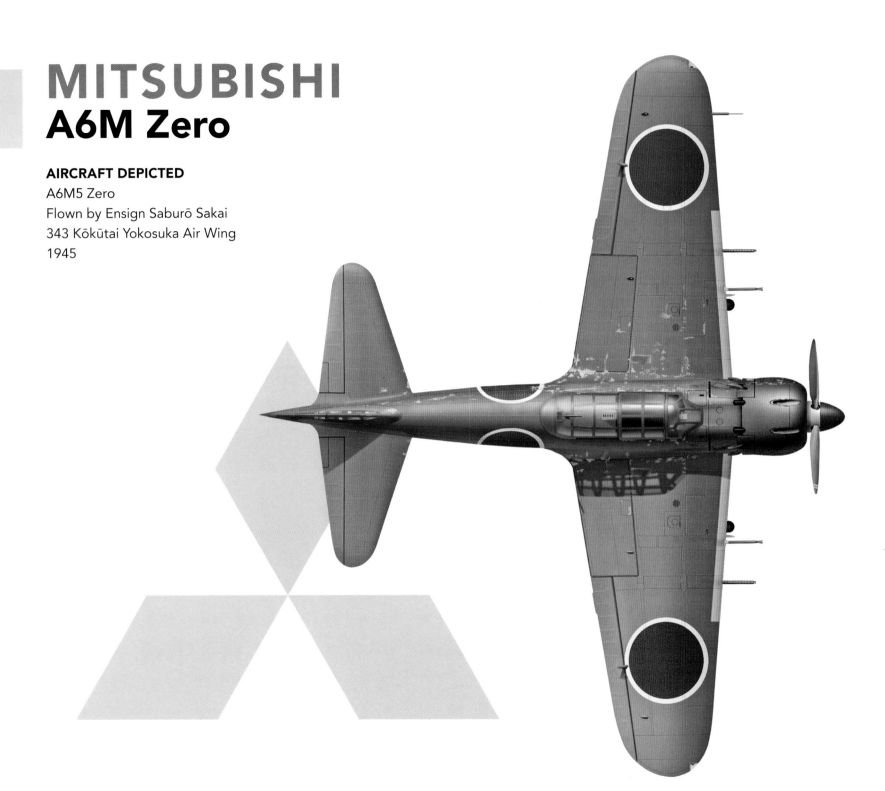

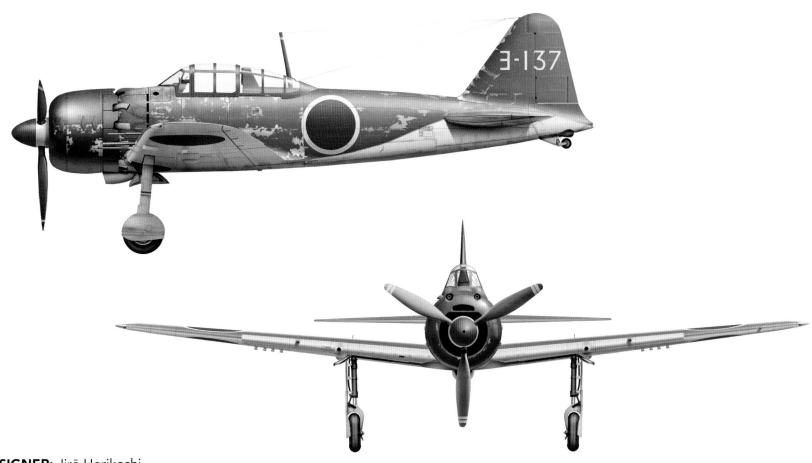

DESIGNER: Jirō Horikoshi
MANUFACTURER: Mitsubishi Heavy Industries Ltd.
AIRFRAMES PRODUCED: 10,939

SPECIFICATIONS

Length . . . . .29 ft 11 in (9.12m)
Wingspan. . . . . 46 ft (14.02m)
Height . . . . 12 ft 5 in (3.78m)
Empty weight. . . . . .4,136 lb (1,876kg)
Loaded weight. . . . . .6,025 lb (2,733kg)
Engine . . . . Nakajima NK1F Sakae 21
Output. . . . . 1,130 hp

Maximum speed . . . . 351 mph (565kmh)
Cruising speed. . . . . 250 mph (402kmh)
Ceiling . . . . 38,520 ft (11,741m)
Range . . . . .1,374 mi (2,211km)
Armament . . . . .7.7mm machine guns × 2
20mm Type 99 cannons × 2

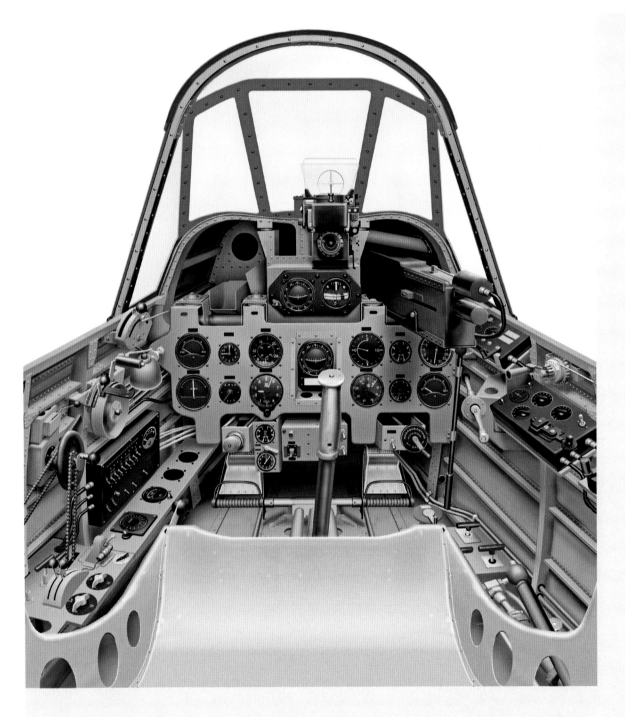

MITSUBISHI A6M Zero

1. Type 98 reflector gunsight
2. Artifical horizon
3. Turn and bank indicator
4. Type 3 13.2mm machine gun
5. High-altitude automatic mixture control
6. Exhaust temperature gauge
7. Clock
8. Airspeed indicator
9. Magnetic compass
10. Rate of climb indicator
11. Fuel and oil pressure gauge
12. Tachometer
13. Emergency fuel pump lever
14. Direction finder control unit
15. Emergency power boost
16. Radio direction indicator
17. Magneto switch
18. Altimeter
19. Control column
20. Manifold pressure gauge
21. Oil temperature gauge
22. Cylinder head temperature gauge
23. Cockpit light

24. Throttle quadrant/20mm
    cannon-firing lever

25. Primer

26. Oxygen-supply gauge

27. Hydraulic pressure gauge

28. 20mm cannon master switch

29. Oil cooler shutter control

30. Cowl flap control

31. Radio control unit

32. Elevator trimming tab control

33. Circuit breakers

34. Rudder pedals

35. Wing tanks cooling
    air-intake control

36. Emergency gear-down lever

37. Loop antenna handle

38. Seat up/down lever

39. Fuel tank jettison handle

40. Fuselage tank fuel gauge

41. Wing tanks fuel gauge

42. Emergency fuel jettison lever

43. Fuselage/wing tanks
    switching cock

44. Wing tank selector lever

45. Bomb release lever

46. Seat

47. Arresting-hook winding wheel

48. Wing tank fuel-switching cock

CHAPTER 5

CURTISS
P-40 Warhawk

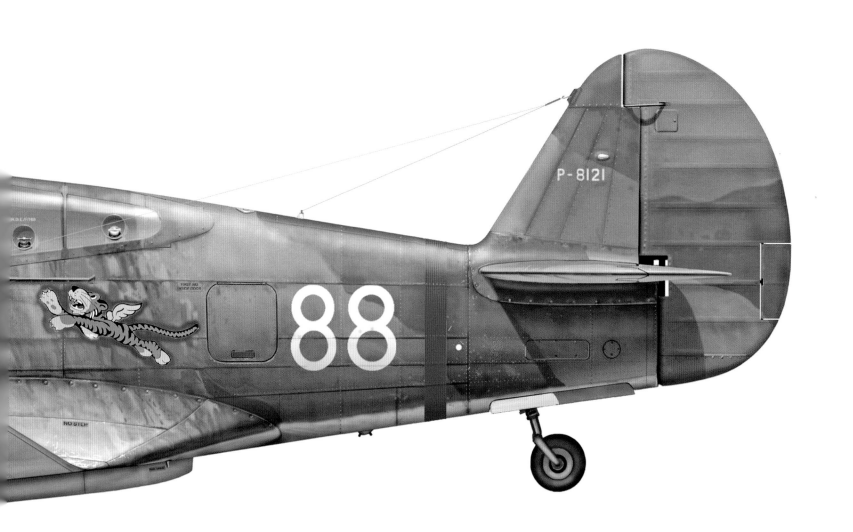

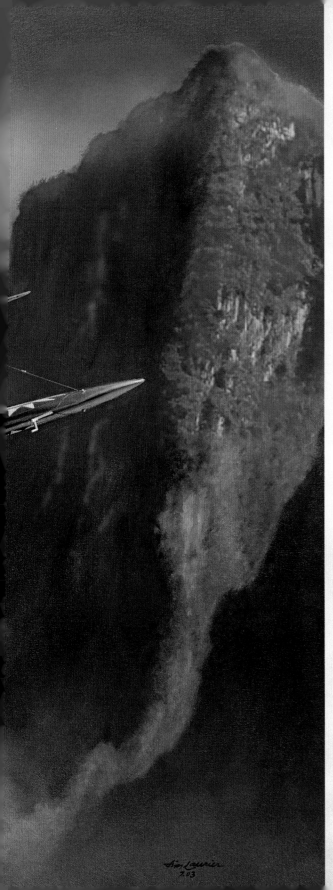

The developmental history of the P-40 Warhawk is unique in that it began its life as another aircraft, the P-36 Hawk, also known as the Curtiss Hawk Model 75. It was one of the first all-metal monoplane fighters in the US inventory, and its first flight was on May 6, 1935. It was the only viable American front-line fighter in 1935.

P-36 performance was above other US designs at the time. Although it was a sturdy and maneuverable aircraft, it was already outclassed by aircraft in Europe and Japan by the late 1930s. America needed a faster and better-equipped fighter.

Aeronautical engineer Donovan R. "Don" Berlin, who had recently joined the Curtiss-Wright Airplane Division, was put in charge of redesigning the P-36 to accept the new Allison liquid-cooled V-12 engine. The goal was to create a fighter that could reach at least 300 miles per hour (483kmh) to become a competitor in the race to secure US Army Air Corps contracts.

The Army Air Corps ordered a test design designated the XP-37: a P-36 airframe mated to an Allison V-1710 engine with 1,000 horsepower and a supercharger. During testing the aircraft became the first US pursuit plane to exceed 300 miles per hour (483kmh). The results were encouraging, and further modifications and testing were made, but the unreliability of the new superchargers eventually resulted in the project being dropped.

Don Berlin pushed ahead in his design work using a modified Allison engine with a P-36A airframe. Initial test data indicated better results, and the Air Corps issued a contract to develop and produce another test aircraft, the XP-40. Mating a liquid-cooled engine to an airframe designed for a radial engine required extensive modifications and redesign. The finished design, however, was a striking aircraft. Unlike the stubby P-36, the XP-40 had a long, pointed front fuselage that tightly enclosed the Allison engine. The new fighter looked sleek and fast just sitting on the ground.

The XP-40's first flight took place on October 14, 1938. In January 1939, the XP-40 was entered into a fighter competition where it easily outperformed all the other designs in the field. The XP-40 reached a speed of 340 miles per hour (547kmh), failing to meet the Air Corps' requirement for a top speed of 360 miles per hour (579kmh). The flight test also indicated a few other problems left to overcome. Berlin and his design team went back to work. Their efforts were rewarded in December 1939 when the XP-40 reached a top speed of 366 miles per hour (589kmh) at 15,000 feet (4,572m).

The P-40 went into production in March 1940 with the designation H-81, which was, in effect, the P-40B. It had two .50-caliber nose-mounted machine guns and one .30-caliber gun in each wing. Changes made during production improved the design, including the addition of a second .30-caliber gun in each wing. Some of the changes were requested by the British, who were now receiving the new fighters to augment RAF efforts against the Germans. The British called the P-40B the Tomahawk I, and most went to North

Tigers in the Pass. P-40B Tomahawks of the American Volunteer Group, or "Flying Tigers," pass between mountainous pillars of karst as they approach their airfield in Kweilin, China. The burned-out wreckage of a Japanese Ki-43 "Oscar" lies in the valley below, victim of a previous engagement with the Tigers.

PREVIOUS PAGES: P-40B Tomahawk flown by Flight Leader Ken Jernstedt, American Volunteer Group, 3rd Squadron, January 1942.

Africa to fight the Luftwaffe and Rommel. In this role, the Tomahawks added bomb shackles and had their wing guns replaced with British .303 guns. P-40Cs were almost identical to the B model with most of the differences in the fuselage: increased fuel capacity, improved radio, and provisions for a droppable external fuel tank.

Extensive redesign and improvements brought about the P-40D and E models. A more powerful Allison V-1710-39 engine gave much better performance at altitude. Modifications to the radiator, air intake, engine, and propeller spinner also gave the P-40 a new look. The canopy glass was redesigned for better visibility, and the four wings guns were swapped for six .50-caliber guns (the two nose-mounted guns were removed). Ammunition capacity was also increased. Landing gear legs were shortened, and the retract mechanism was improved. Finally, the mechanical gun-charging handles were replaced by a much more reliable hydraulic charging system.

The P-40F was the first variant to use the British Rolls-Royce Merlin engine, a modification that warranted a developmental testing period similar to the prototypes. The Rolls-Royce gave the airplane improved performance and enabled it to carry a heavier bomb load and more fuel. The F carried six .50-caliber wing guns. Only 1,312 of this type were built.

The P-40K was a further development of the E model equipped with a powerful Allison V-170-73 (F4R) engine. The extra power gave the aircraft a tendency to swing on takeoff, so a dorsal fin extension was added forward of the vertical stabilizer to counter this effect. The later K models had their fuselages extended. K models had a strengthened forward canopy and automatic engine boost control. Along with some E models, some K models were modified for winter service in the Aleutian Islands.

The P-40L, M, and N models were modifications aimed at improving overall performance. Starting with the Merlin-powered L, major effort was put into

BELOW LEFT: One of the first all-metal monoplane fighters in the US inventory, the P-40 made its first flight on May 6, 1935.

BELOW: The first American ace of World War II was made in a P-40 when 1st Lt. Boyd "Buzz" Wagner downed his fifth Japanese aircraft on December 16, 1941.

ABOVE: Australia's highest-scoring ace, Clive Caldwell, scored 22 of his 28.5 kills in a P-40.

RIGHT: An American Volunteer Group P-40 undergoes maintenance in Kunming, China, circa 1941. Note the unique roundel painted on the wheel's hub.

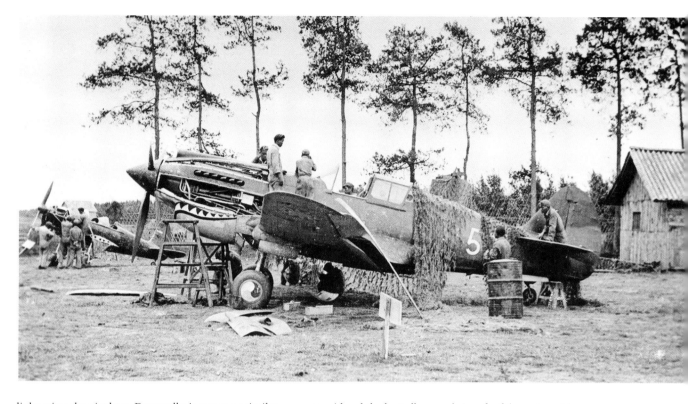

lightening the airplane. Externally, it was very similar to the long-fuselage F model, but with only four wing guns. Some L models could carry wing-mounted rockets, as well. The P-40M went back to the Allison V-1710-81 engine and six .50-caliber wing guns. All M models had the long-fuselage design.

The final, and probably best, P-40 production design was the N. Numerous modifications improved the type, with speed and weight the primary considerations. The N used the Allison V-1710-81 and carried four .50-caliber wing guns. It had a frameless sliding canopy glass and a cut-down rear cockpit deck for optimum visibility. Some features that lightened the aircraft included smaller wheels, the removal of two guns and front-wing fuel tanks, and aluminum oil coolers and radiators instead of brass. Later production models had two more wing guns added for a total of six. Additional improvements included a better radio, navigation, and oxygen systems. The N was the most-produced P-40, with 5,219 airframes built. It was

considered the best all-around aircraft of the series with a top speed of 378 miles per hour (608kmh).

The P-40 was the third-most-produced US aircraft at 16,800 airframes.

★ ★ ★

One might wonder why the P-40 should be selected as one of best fighter aircraft of World War II. It wasn't the fastest or the most innovative. It was, in fact, a somewhat outdated and simple airplane compared to many other fighters of the period. But it was a steadfast and reliable workhorse. It was also fairly easy to fly, and like other great fighters, a lethal weapon in the hands of a good pilot.

The P-40 was an aircraft of many firsts. It was the first mass-produced fighter. It was the fighter that first engaged America's enemies in World War II. The very first American ace of the war was made in a P-40 when 1st Lt. Boyd "Buzz" Wagner downed his fifth Japanese

aircraft on December 16, 1941. During the Japanese attacks on Pearl Harbor, the P-40 was the first air defense when 2nd Lt. George Welch downed four Japanese planes with his P-40. Kenneth Taylor downed three more with his P-40. Almost every Allied country flew the P-40 in every type of climate. Australia's highest scoring ace, Clive "Killer" Caldwell, scored 22 of his 28.5 kills in a P-40.

Certainly, the big factor that helped cement the P-40's place in history was the American Volunteer Group (AVG) in China in 1941. The AVG, or Flying Tigers, as they became known, flew the P-40 against the Japanese before the United States was officially in the war. A special arrangement was made with US ally China that allowed Americans to fly P-40s for pay in an attempt to thwart Japan's efforts to grab huge

swaths of territory in China and surrounding regions. Under the skilled leadership of Gen. Claire Chennault, the AVG achieved an impressive combat record in a very short period of time. With a loss of only twelve aircraft in combat, the Flying Tigers were credited with destroying almost three hundred Japanese aircraft from December 21, 1941, to July 6, 1942. That is a kill ratio of seventy to one that has never been matched. Though an impressive record, what was more important was the destruction of the perception that the Japanese were invincible—a perception held by many Chinese and Americans, as well as the Japanese themselves. This was a huge boost to America's morale and a wakeup call to the Japanese, a hint of the kind of fight they could expect from America for the rest of the war.

Tiger Dawn. During their tenure in China, the American Volunteer Group (AVG), or "Flying Tigers," as they were better known, operated from various airfields in southern China. One of these bases was in Wujiaba, where they were stationed from early 1942 to July 1942.

This image shows two well-known Third Squadron "Hell's Angels," Robert "R. T." Smith and Charles "Chuck" Older, as they take off from Wujiaba on an early morning in June 1942 for a raid on a Japanese airfield. It is warm and humid as morning fog and mist lift to create a hazy view of the mountains in the distance.

RIGHT: This lineup of thirteen P-40 Warhawks has just been presented to French forces at an airport somewhere in North Africa. Note the Lafayette Escadrille insignia painted on the fuselages—a nod to the World War I French Air Service fighter squadron comprising mostly American pilots.

As the first mass-produced American fighter of World War II, the P-40 carried the burden of war on every front until production of superior types could get up to speed. The P-40 was thought to be outclassed by all its adversaries. The Mitsubishi Zero was far better in many ways, as were the Bf 109 and Fw 190. Whatever the P-40 seemed to lack in overall performance (interestingly, it could outmaneuver the Bf 109 and the P-51 Mustang) was offset by its rugged construction and survivability in combat.

In 2002 Patrick Masell compared the Zero to the P-40. An excerpt from his article gives a clear example of the P-40's survivability:

> Clive Caldwell, Australia's top-scoring ace with 28½ victories and the leading P-40 ace with 20½ of these victories, demonstrated this rather dramatically in North Africa.
>
> While flying top cover for supply planes inbound for Tobruk, two Bf-109s led by the 114-victory ace Werner Schroer ambushed him. The German

planes punched 108 machine gun bullets and five 20mm shells into the hapless fighter, damaging its instrument panel, controls, tail, wings, and wounding Caldwell in the back, shoulder and leg.

> Instead of crashing to the ground, the Tomahawk managed to stay airborne. And instead of attempting to escape, the Sydney-born Caldwell turned into his attackers and returned fire. He shot down Schroer's wingman, unnerving Schroer to the point that he ran for home. The Australian ace made it home.

When pilots used the right tactics, the P-40 was a good match for any of the more advanced enemy fighters. It was a very good gun platform, with six .50-caliber machine guns able to destroy anything in the air or on the ground, and it could outdive any of its enemy contemporaries. And the simplicity of the P-40 was actually one of its best virtues, as it was easy to build, maintain, and repair.

ABOVE: A Chinese soldier guards a line of American P-40 fighters, painted with the shark-face emblem of the Flying Tigers. Aircraft No. 106 is a P-40E piloted by Maj. John Emil Petach, who was killed on July 10, 1942, a few days after this photo was taken. A flight leader with the 2nd "Panda Bear" Squadron (later 75th Fighter Squadron, 23rd Fighter Group), Petach accumulated 5.25 kills.

RIGHT: ***Oscar Valley.*** P-40Ns of the 75th Fighter Squadron, 23rd Fighter Group, engage Ki-43 Oscars of the 48th Sentai near Heng Shan, China. This fight occurred at low altitude on the morning of August 8, 1944, and varied from 1,000 feet altitude to treetop level at various times. The P-40N in the foreground, piloted by Maj. Don Quigley, made several head-on passes at one particular Oscar; he scored hits each time, but the Oscar managed to break off and finally evade Quigley's fire. Quigley ran out of ammunition and broke off his attack, never seeing his prey go down.

As with most aircraft, pilots had different impressions of the P-40. Most saw it for what it was: a dray horse rather than a thoroughbred, as one pilot put it. But a dray horse is useful, too, as the P-40 proved.

In Eric Bergerud's book *Fire in the Sky: The Air War in the South Pacific*, P-40 ace Joel Paris commented:

> I never felt I was a second-class citizen in a P-40. In many ways I thought the P-40 was better than the more modern fighters. I had a hell of a lot of time in a P-40, probably close to a thousand hours. I could make it sit up and talk. It was an unforgiving airplane. It had vicious stall characteristics . . . If you knew what you were doing, you could fight a Jap on even terms, but you had to make him fight your way. . . . You could push things, too. Because you knew one thing: If you decided to go home, you could go home. He couldn't because you could outrun him. He couldn't even leave the fight because you were faster. That left you in control.

It should be noted that Paris's comments about the P-40 being unforgiving pertained mostly to the early B and C models. Those variants needed constant pilot attention to maintain proper flight control, particularly in maneuvers. With improvements in later variants, the P-40 became more manageable, although every type was effective for a pilot who mastered it.

Despite some negative impressions of the P-40, it most often surprised its adversaries when flown by an aggressive pilot using proven tactics. P-40s did very well when the aircraft's superior diving speed was used in an attack. Masell quotes Saburō Sakai, Japan's leading ace to survive World War II, regarding an encounter with P-40 pilot Les Jackson:

> We passed Moresby [New Guinea] and the bursting flak fell behind. I sighed with relief. Too soon! Nearly a mile above us, a single P-40 fighter dove with incredible speed. He came down so fast I could not move a muscle; one second he

was above us, the next the lone plane plummeted like lightning into the bombers. Six hundred yards in front of me, I watched the fighter—he was going to ram! How that plane ever got through the few yards' clearance between the third and fourth bombers of the left echelon, I shall never know. It seemed impossible, but it happened. With all guns blazing, the P-40 ripped through the bomber formation and poured a river of lead into Miyazaki's plane. Instantly the Zero burst into flames. With tremendous speed the P-40 disappeared far below.

Many other countries used the P-40, most notably the Soviet Union, which received over 2,600 examples

P-40N *Geronimo* was flown by 1st Lt. Bruce Campbell of the 45th Fighter Squadron, 15th Fighter Group. The aircraft, painted a sand color, is being serviced at Makin Island in the Gilbert Islands in 1943. This Warhawk later became the basis for at least one plastic model kit.

ABOVE: A P-40 of the 11th Fighter Squadron, 343rd Fighter Group, shows off its "Aleutian tiger" nose art as it prepares to take off from a base in Alaska.

RIGHT: Landing wheels recede as a USAAF Liberator bomber crosses the shark-nosed bows of P-40 fighter planes at an advanced US base in China, circa 1943.

of the fighter. Other countries that used the P-40 were Australia, Brazil, Canada, China, Egypt, Finland, France, Indonesia, Netherlands, New Zealand, Poland, South Africa, Turkey, and the United Kingdom.

Usually overshadowed by more famous and glamorous types such as the P-51 Mustang and Supermarine Spitfire, the P-40 did not receive much attention by the press and little praise was ever given to it. The exception was its brief time in the limelight resulting from its early success in China with the AVG. In 1942, the remnants of the AVG reformed into the 23rd Fighter Group, which became one of the most successful fighter units of World War II.

The ubiquitous P-40 enjoyed many successes throughout the majority of the war in every combat theater as it humbly fought on in relative obscurity. It was essential to the defense of the many regions in which it operated. The passage of time has allowed a more accurate assessment of its true value. Perhaps the P-40's significance is realized more today than it was during World War II, but its fame and legendary status was hard won—and the P-40 earned every bit of it.

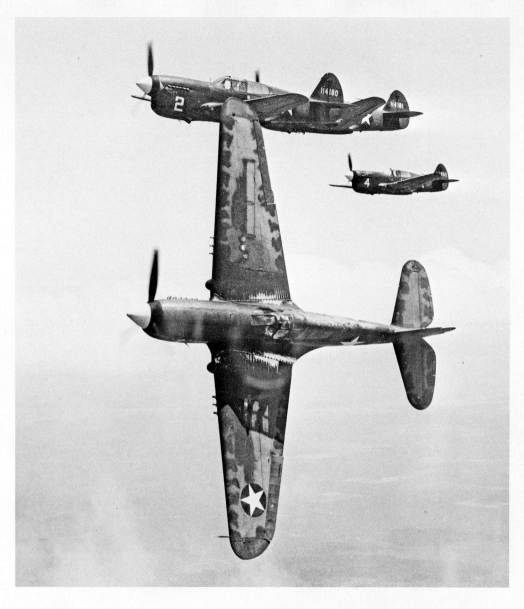

ABOVE: US Army Air Force P-40Fs on a training flight out of Moore Field, near Mission, Texas, in 1943. The lead aircraft is peeling off for a practice attack. Selected aviation cadets received transition training in P-40s before receiving their wings.

OPPOSITE: **Snow Tiger, Red Dragon.** P-40 E Warhawks of the 343rd Fighter Group begin their dive into a formation of Japanese Mitsubishi GM3 "Nell" bombers and Mitsubishi Zero fighters headed for a bombing raid on Dutch Harbor, Alaska. War in the Aleutian Islands came with the additional hardship of severe weather conditions, particularly for air operations. Storms and heavy fog could appear suddenly. Finding a downed pilot could be dangerous, and the climate on land and at sea lessened the pilot's chances of being rescued in time.

©Jim Laurier

CURTISS
P-40 Warhawk

AIRCRAFT DEPICTED

P-40M Warhawk
Flown by Lieutenant James Lee
75th Squadron, 23rd Fighter Group
Kunming, China
Late summer, 1943

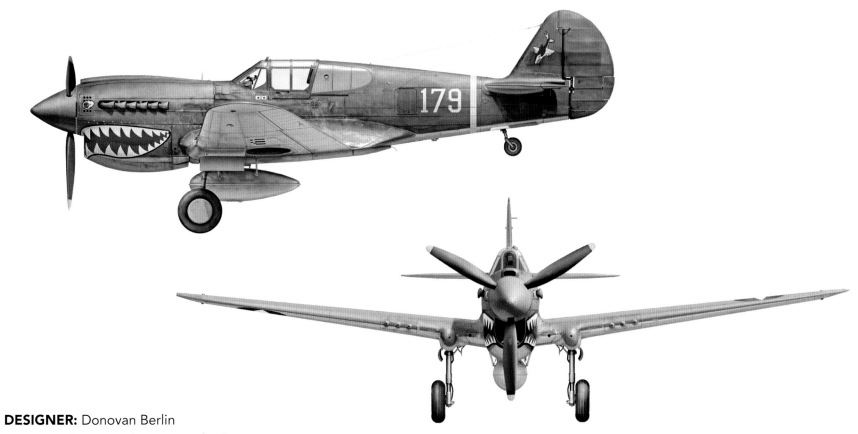

DESIGNER: Donovan Berlin
MANUFACTURER: Curtiss-Wright Corporation
AIRFRAMES PRODUCED: 16,800

SPECIFICATIONS

Length . . . . .33 ft 6 in (10.21m)	Output. . . . . 1,360 hp
Wingspan. . . . . 37 ft 3.5 in (11.37m)	Maximum speed . . . . 378 mph (608kmh)
Height . . . . 12 ft 4.5 in (3.77m)	Cruising speed. . . . . 277 mph (446kmh)
Empty weight. . . . . .6,200 lb (2,812kg)	Ceiling . . . . 38,156 ft (11,630m)
Loaded weight. . . . . .8,350 lb (3,788kg)	Range . . . . .276 mi (444km)
Engine . . . . Allison V-1710-81	Armament . . . . .50-caliber machine guns × 6

CURTISS
P-40 Warhawk

1. N-3A reflector gunsight
2. Ring gunsight
3. Flap and wheel indicator
4. Compass
5. Flight indicator
6. Coolant temperature gauge
7. Fuselage fuel gauge
8. Turn and bank indicator
9. Turn indicator
10. Airspeed indicator
11. Tachometer
12. Manifold pressure gauge
13. Oil temperature gauge
14. Engine gauge unit
15. Rate of climb indicator
16. Altimeter
17. Oxygen indicator
18. Oxygen pressure gauge
19. Oil pressure gauge
20. Fuel pressure gauge
21. Parking brake
22. Gun arming switch
23. Warning lights
24. Carburetor heat control
25. Canopy control crank
26. Throttle

27. Mixture control
28. Propeller control
29. Ignition switch
30. Compass control
31. Ammeter
32. Cockpit heat control
33. Rudder trim control tab
34. Elevator trim control tab
35. Fuel selector
36. Rudder pedals
37. Control stick
38. Gun firing button
39. Forward wing tank fuel gauge
40. Hydraulics hand pump
41. Radio receiver
42. Radio transmitter
43. Map case
44. Fluorescent spotlight
45. Wing bomb release
46. Pilot's seat
47. Cowl flaps control switch
48. Radio crash switch
49. Filter switch box
50. Fluorescent spotlight
51. Oxygen regulator
52. Oxygen hose
53. Flap selector
54. Undercarriage selector handle

CHAPTER 6

FOCKE-WULF
Fw 190

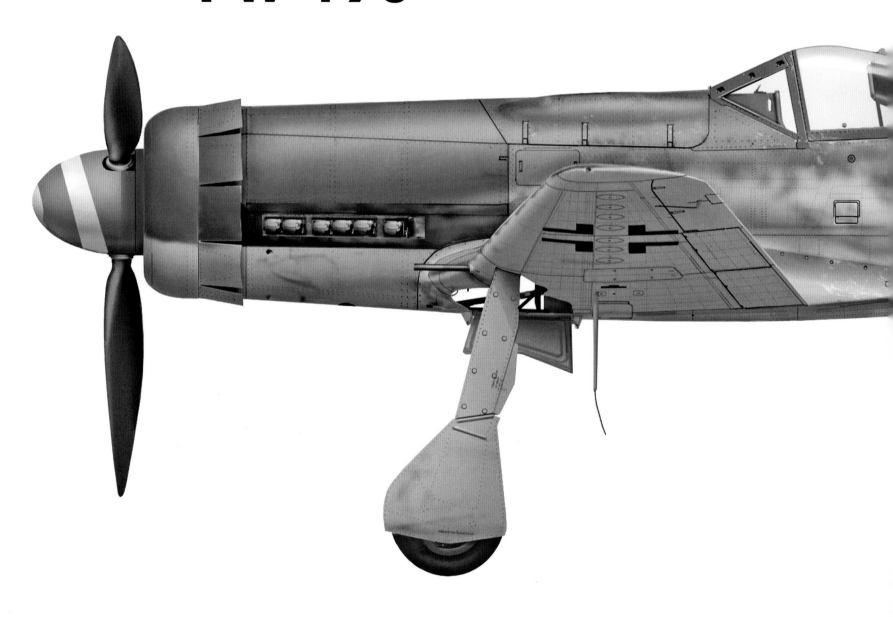

Early in World War II, the Reichsluftfahrtministerium (German Air Ministry, abbreviated RLM) was looking for another fighter to support the very successful Messerschmitt Bf 109. The German military strategy at the time hinged on the concept of blitzkrieg, or "lightning war," by which enemies could be conquered in a matter of weeks rather than months. Fighter aircraft were used strictly as offensive weapons and were designed with very streamlined profiles and new, powerful V-12 engines that allowed them to use speed and surprise to quickly overwhelm and defeat the enemy.

One of the firms competing to win the contract for the new fighter was the Focke-Wulf Flugzeugbau AG. The head of the design office at Focke-Wulf was Dipl.-Ing. (Diplom-Ingenieur, or certified engineer) Kurt Tank. He proposed a new radial engine fighter that would surpass the Bf 109 in performance.

The RLM didn't believe that a radial-engined fighter would be adequate for blitzkrieg tactics and were at first reluctant to accept Tank's design proposal. However, they realized that radial engines were easier to build, operate, and maintain than inline engines, and were known to be more resistant to battle damage. In addition, the production of radial engines would not interfere with V-12 engine production, which would be needed to meet the ever-increasing demands for V-12-powered aircraft.

Focke-Wulf was given a contract to design a new, single-seat, low-wing monoplane that would be employed as a defensive superiority fighter. To appease the RLM, Tank initially presented two proposals: one using the Daimler-Benz DB 601 V-12 and one with the BMW 139 radial engine. The RLM accepted Tank's design using the BMW 139 air-cooled radial engine, and as plans went forward, Tank continued experimenting with V-12 designs.

A primary figure on Tank's design team was Hans Sander, an aeronautical engineer and highly regarded test pilot. Together, they began work immediately creating a new fighter that would be called the Focke-Wulf Fw 190. The basic concept was to build a fighter around the small-profile BMW radial engine enclosed in a tight-fitting, low-drag cowling and mated to a compact and very robust airframe. It would be of all-metal construction with fabric-covered control surfaces, with most of the aircraft systems electrically actuated rather than relying on more vulnerable hydraulic systems. The Fw 190 was designed to be built and serviced easily. The subassemblies could be produced at separate locations by subcontractors and transported elsewhere for assembly. Easy access to the engine and weapons systems would be accomplished by incorporating hinged access panels that could also be completely removed.

Bretschneider's End. On Christmas Eve 1944, Luftwaffe ace Klaus Bretschneider of V./JG 300 participated in an attack on B-24 bombers over Kassel, Germany. Near Hausen, Bretschneider was caught from behind by a P-51 Mustang of the 357th Fighter Group and shot down. He went down with his Fw-190A-8 *Red 1* and crashed near Hessen. By this time he had claimed thirty-four enemy aircraft, mostly heavy bombers. Fourteen of his victories were achieved at night while flying with a Wilde Sau (literally, "Wild Boar") night-fighter unit.

PREVIOUS PAGES: Ta-152 H-1/R11 flown by Oberfeldwebel Willi Reschke, Stab 301, Neustadt-Glewe, Germany, March 1945.

The first drawings were completed in July 1938, and in spring 1939, the first prototype, Fw 190V-1 (V for *versuch*, or research) was completed. The first flight occurred on June 1, 1939, with Sander as the test pilot. He reported that the airplane handled extremely well, but there were problems with engine overheating and excessive heat and exhaust fumes in the cockpit caused by the lack of cooling fans behind the propeller (the fan design had not been completed in time for the first flight). The cooling blades were installed on aircraft V-1, but problems persisted with the motor on this and several subsequent test models until numerous design updates were made.

Modifications and testing continued with the initial V models, the V-5 bringing some significant improvements. The BMW 139 motor was swapped for the more powerful BMW 801C, along with some other changes: lengthened and strengthened fuselage, redesigned cowling, longer wingspan, better cooling fan, and redesigned cheek bulges, which housed the air ducts leading to the supercharger and rear engine cylinders. The early Fw 190Vs and As had four machine guns: two MG 17 7.9-millimeter guns in the cowling and two MG 131 13-millimeter guns in the wings.

Numerous alterations occurred during development, but the 190 still experienced myriad problems, including continued engine overheating to the extent that the RLM considered scrapping the whole project. Tank's persistence and skillful negotiating with BMW and the RLM, however, kept the dream alive while the plane cut its teeth. Eventually all of the more serious issues were resolved.

In early 1940 the preproduction A series made its way onto the factory airfields for testing. A group of experienced pilots was formed to perform test flights on the Fw 190 while modifications and planning for full-scale manufacturing continued throughout 1940. The A series of test aircraft had the BMW 801C engines and, beginning with the A-2, a pair of MG 151 cannons mounted in the wing roots. Some A-1 and A-2 models

were equipped with a slightly more powerful BMW 801D engine.

In the spring of 1941, the first Fw 190A-1s had completed their testing, during which many small refinements were made to satisfy the Air Ministry sufficiently to proceed with production and dispersal to combat units. By September 1941, II Gruppe/JG 26 had traded their Bf 109Es for Fw 190A-1s and had seen their first combat with RAF Spitfires, besting the British aircraft without losing any of their own. This completely surprised and shocked the British, who had not seen this fighter before and were not sure what it was. In his book *Fight for the Sky*, legendary RAF leader Douglas Bader recalled the effect of the new fighter's debut: "At first, we were told that the Jerries must have got hold of some old Curtiss aeroplanes, and we said 'If that's the case, could we get some of those old Curtiss aeroplanes, please?'"

An abandoned Fw 190A-8 "White 21" near Nuremberg. The fuselage bands look like the red and yellow of JG 301. The two hood-mounted machine guns are missing, and it appears to have partial 20-millimeter ammo belts draped over the windscreen. Some of the sheep apparently find it useful for shade.

The Fw 190 would outclass all the RAF had in inventory until the first Spitfire Mk IX arrived, which could match the Fw 190's performance, except in turns.

In mid-1942 A-3 models were introduced with BMW 801D-1 and D-2 engines. A centerline bomb rack was added to carry either a bomb or external fuel tank. Variants with this configuration were called "Jabos," or fighter-bombers, and were used in a ground-attack role. The A-3 brought with it an increase in subvariant conversions. Rocket tubes, underwing bomb racks, tropicalized air intakes, reconnaissance cameras, wing gun cameras, and mods for high-altitude operation were some of the conversions.

Inevitably, an intact example of an Fw 190 eventually fell into British hands. The Air Fighting Development Unit eagerly dissected and tested the strange new fighter to discover all its secrets. One of Britain's foremost test pilots, Lt. Eric Brown, commented, "I recall clearly the excitement with which I first examined the Focke-Wulf fighter; the impression of elegant lethality that its functional yet pleasing lines exuded. To me it represented the very quintessence of aeronautical pulchritude from any angle. It was not to my eye, more beautiful than the Spitfire, but its beauty took a different form—the contrast being such as that between a blonde and brunette!"

Fw 190A-4 had improved radio equipment, and the engine-cooling slats on the side of the cowling were replaced with adjustable gills. MW 50 water-methanol engine injection was used on some aircraft for war emergency power. New Rüstsätze field conversion kits were made available for adapting the aircraft to varying tactical uses.

The Fw 190A-5 had its forward fuselage extended forward 6 inches, just ahead of the wing roots, among

Allied personnel examine a damaged Fw 190A-4 of III. Gruppe **Schnellkampfgeschwader** 10 (III./SKG 10, 3rd Group, 10th Fast Bomber Wing) at El Aouina airport in Tunis, Tunisia, in May 1943.

ABOVE: A captured Fw 190 is shown in flight near Naval Air Station Patuxent River, Maryland, in 1944. The aircraft is painted in overall red and has USAAF star-and-bar insignia painted in the four usual locations. This aircraft looks to be in very good condition, except for some paint wear under the cockpit from pilots climbing in and out.

OPPOSITE: *Winter Wulf.* In the winter of 1942–1943, the Luftwaffe enjoyed aerial supremacy over the Soviets on the Eastern Front. Most Soviet fighters were inferior to German designs, and many top Luftwaffe aces racked up very high tallies. As newer and better Soviet aircraft and better-trained pilots began arriving in theater, the arena became slightly more even, but the Germans most often came out on top. In this scene, Fw 190s of the JG 54 "Green Hearts" have caught a squadron of Soviet I-15 Ratas in the landing pattern at the air base somewhere in the Leningrad sector.

other more detailed refinements. Further changes that came with the Fw 190A-6, A-7, and A-8 were partly due to all the previous revisions that had resulted in an increase in weight. Most notable was a strengthening of the wings beginning with the A-6. The hood-mounted 7.92-millimeter MG 17 guns were replaced with 13-millimeter MG 131s. A bulged hood panel was used to cover the larger guns, and an improved REVI 16B gunsight assisted in aiming the new weapons. On some later A series fighters, a conversion set offered for attacking bombers used two Mk 108 30-millimeter cannons housed one each in underwing gondolas. Some A-6s and A-7s were used as Sturmjäger fighters and had armor cockpit

glass and metal cockpit side armor. These were employed later in the war in a desperate attempt to stop the relentless streams of Allied bombers over Germany.

The Fw 190F series was intended as a ground-attack aircraft. The main differences from previous versions were the addition of added armor protection under the cowling, cockpit, and fuselage fuel cells. F series aircraft had only wing-root MG 151 cannon and hood-mounted machine guns. Bomb racks were installed under the outer wings, two on each side. A bulged, or "blown," canopy glass was added for better visibility.

The G-1 through G-8 carried only two wing-root MG 151 cannons, with the hood-mounted guns removed. Some were configured for night-fighter operations, and others carried faired-in underwing 300l fuel tanks for long-range ground-attack missions.

As the war progressed, Germany was defending itself on every front against ground forces. To try to stem the tide, Ju 87 Stuka dive-bombers were replaced in the ground-attack role with faster and equally effective Fw 190 Jabos. As these missions became more important, bomber pilots were recruited to fly Fw 190s. To help pilots transition to these missions, some Fw 190s were modified into two-seat trainers, called Schulflugzeug, or S models. Only a few were built and issued to training units, however.

The final Fw 190 variant was so significantly different than all its predecessors that it should be considered a different aircraft. The Fw 190D ("Dora") series was a more updated, refined version of the earlier variants mated to a 2,060-horsepower Junkers Jumo 213A liquid-cooled, inverted V-12 engine. Development and testing of the long-nosed Fw 190s using the inline engine was conducted as early as 1942 with the B and C series. Though superior to the BMW 801 motors, the earlier inline engines fell short of the desired performance at higher altitudes.

The V-12 concept was revisited with more purposeful intent in the latter part of the war as newer Allied fighters outperformed the radial-engined 190s, all of which were still giving the Allies plenty of headaches in the air and on the ground. Kurt Tank wanted to surpass or at least match the best Allied fighters, and he proved he could do so when the first Fw 190D appeared in August 1944.

Fw 190Ds incorporated many large and small changes to make the design into what would become the greatest piston-powered Luftwaffe fighter of World War II. The fuselage was lengthened aft of the cockpit to restore the center of gravity offset by the added length and weight in the nose. Various armament configurations were used, such as a Mk 108 30-millimeter cannons firing through the nose, two MG 131 guns on the hood, and two wing-mounted MG 151 cannons.

P-51 Mustang and late-mark Spitfire pilots, having adjusted to fighting the Fw 190A and F models, were now presented with another nasty surprise. The Fw 190D was instantly loved by those who flew it—and hated by those who opposed it. For the Luftwaffe, however, it was a case of too little, too late. Fw 190Ds were produced in fairly good numbers but saw limited combat due to lack of fuel and other resources as the war drew to a close. Compounding difficulties were the lack of experienced pilots and inadequate training time for new pilots. Many Doras were assigned to fly top cover for Me 262 jet fighters, which were vulnerable to attack during landings and takeoffs.

The last Fw 190 design was the "Ta" series (for Tank, in tribute to its designer). The Ta was the result of further development of the D model. It used either the Jumo 213F or a Daimler-Benz DB 603 and had two wing-mounted MG 151 cannons and one Mk 108 cannon in the nose. There were a few variants of the type—the A, B, C, and H—but attention was focused on the H (Hoehenjaeger, or High-Altitude Fighter), meant to serve as an interceptor. Its wingspan was extended to 47 feet 7 inches (14.5m), and it was powered by a Jumo 213E with a three-speed supercharger. The H model was also the first single-seat fighter to have a pressurized cabin. It entered service in January 1945, with very few seeing any combat action.

The Fw 190 was used by a few foreign countries: Turkey, 1942–1949; France, 1945–1949; Hungary, 1944–1945; Romania, 1944–1945; Poland, 1945; and Yugoslavia, 1944–1946.

★ ★ ★

As one of the Luftwaffe's two most prolific frontline fighters, the Focke-Wulf Fw 190 served in a number of offensive and defensive roles. Early on, it was used over the English Channel and on the Eastern Front as an offensive weapon, but for the majority of the war it

ABOVE: Luftwaffe ace Oskar Bösch served in JG 3, flying the Fw 190A-8 Sturmjäger, a heavily armed and armor-reinforced version of the Fw 190 used against bombers.

OPPOSITE: *JG 2.* Early in the war, US heavy bombers flew deep into Germany with partial protection from American fighters, which lacked the range to escort bombers for an entire flight. Luftwaffe fighters would wait until they saw the US escort fighters turn for home and then swoop in to attack. Here, Egon Mayer of JG 2 sweeps through a formation of B-17Fs high over Germany.

Jim Laurier ASAA
11.99

was deployed on all fronts as a defensive weapon against bombers, fighters, shipping, and ground forces.

In the defensive role, the Fw 190 was quite remarkable in its adaptability and effectiveness. Its robust construction and formidable firepower were two of its best characteristics, and it would often bring its pilots home from combat after receiving heavy damage. There are accounts of Fw 190s flying back to their bases with an entire engine cylinder blown off or huge holes in the fuselage or wing.

I have spoken with some Luftwaffe pilots about their experiences in the war, in particular asking them about their impressions of the aircraft they flew and those they fought against.

In 1991 Luftwaffe ace Oskar Bösch spoke to me about his memories of the war. Bösch served in JG 3, flying Fw 190A-8 Sturmjägers, heavily armed and armor-reinforced versions used against bombers and sometimes called Rammjägers. Sturmjäger Fw 190s had two Mk 108 30-millimeter cannons in the wing roots and two MG 151 hood-mounted cannons, which were the approximate equivalent of the .50-caliber US machine gun.

Bösch reported that pilots in his unit were told they had to bring down at least one bomber on every mission, by any means possible. If they ran out of ammunition, they were to ram the bombers. He admitted that the hardest, and least desired, task for a Luftwaffe pilot was to attack B-17 and B-24 bombers because of the tremendous firepower each bomber wielded—at least twelve to fourteen .50-caliber machine guns that could be fired in overlapping fields of fire.

German pilots estimated their odds of surviving one firing pass through the massed fire of a bomber formation were fifty-fifty. They also had to contend with US fighter escorts. Their preferred tactic was to attack from behind and slightly above, trying to take out the rear gunner first. Then they would aim for the wing-root fuel tank before rolling their fighter away and down to escape. Bösch was shot down eight times in

Fw 190s and flew back four times in severely damaged airplanes, each time managing to crash-land in grassy areas. On his last mission, he rammed a Russian Yak fighter over Berlin and survived.

Bösch's experiences are proof enough of the durability of the Fw 190. Very few, if any, aircraft could survive ramming other aircraft or the firepower of dozens of .50-caliber guns and manage to fly home. This ruggedness is reminiscent of the American P-47 Thunderbolt and Russian Il-2 Sturmovik, though it was smaller and lighter than either of those aircraft.

World War II aircraft underwent many design improvements during development and production, but probably none more so than the Fw 190. It was continuously refined throughout the war and could be modified with numerous Rüstsätze field conversion kits that could easily be added to the airplane on the front. In addition, the BMW 801 engine was designed to be

This booklet entitled "The Hunter's Shooting Primer" features a stylized Fw 190 on the tail of what appears to be a similarly stylized British fighter aircraft.

ABOVE: Adolf Galland flew various German fighters from 1937 to 1945. He primarily used the Bf 109 but also commanded a small Fw 190 unit for a short time, which gave him experience with that aircraft.

RIGHT: An Fw 190A-8 aircraft "White 11," flown by Gefreiter Walter Wagner of JG 4, participated in the attack on US airfields on January 1, 1945, known as Operation Bodenplatte. This was one of the Luftwaffe's last large-scale operations intended to wipe out Allied aircraft on the ground. Wagner apparently became disoriented during the battle and accidentally landed at the US-held field at St. Trond; the Focke-Wulf was repaired and put back into service with an all-red paint job, US markings, and mock fuselage codes. Note the infamous date of the attack painted on the tail.

quickly replaced in the field by making the cowling, exhaust, supercharger, and most of its plumbing and auxiliary systems removable as a single unit. Kurt Tank designed his fighter to be not only lethal, but practical and functional, with every detail from nose to tail given careful attention.

This practical approach was also evident in the cockpit area. Controls and instruments were very neatly laid out on the main panels and the consoles left and right, plus it was roomier and more comfortable than the Bf 109 and other types. Visibility through the flat armored windscreen and blown canopy was very good. The pilot sat with his legs more or less straight out, which was comfortable and helped counter the effects of g-forces on the upper body. The REVI gunsight was dependable and helped direct accurate fire. The Fw 190 was very responsive to control inputs, but control stick forces could be stiff at higher speeds. It had a roll rate of 160 degrees per second, the highest of any fighter aircraft

of the war, an advantage in breaking away when an enemy fighter got behind you.

I had a chance to meet Luftwaffe General Adolf Galland, who flew various German fighters from 1937 to 1945. His primary mount was the Bf 109, but he commanded a small Fw 190 unit for a short time and flew the Fw 190. His impression of the Fw 190 was that it was a much sturdier airplane than the Bf 109 and a better weapons platform. He said that either aircraft was good in the hands of competent pilots.

In 1997, Colin Heaton published an article in *World War II* magazine about his interview with Galland, in which the general stated, "I had been telling Hitler for over a year, since my first flight in an Me-262, that only Focke Wulf Fw-190 fighter production should continue in conventional aircraft, to discontinue the Me-109, which was outdated, and to focus on building a massive jet-fighter force."

This was generally the view of other Luftwaffe pilots I met, most of whom flew Bf 109s, but who also clearly

recognized the differences between the two. The consensus was that the 109 was better for dogfighting, especially at higher altitudes, but the 190 may have been a slightly better all-around aircraft, less susceptible to battle damage, capable of carrying a heavier weapons payload, and offering much better ground-handling characteristics, which was an advantage to newer pilots. The number of Bf 109s lost or damaged in ground accidents was quite high. The Fw 190, on the other hand, could withstand a bit of rough handling on the ground.

Günther Rall scored 275 aerial victories with the Bf 109, most on the Eastern Front against Soviet pilots. I met him a few times over the years and he recalled air combat in vivid detail. He preferred the 109F over the Fw 190 and even other 109s, but felt the 190 was a good airplane, very rugged, and had very good firepower located around the cowling (on the hood and wing roots). In 2003, he was invited to lecture at the Aviation Museum Society in Finland. The lecture was recorded by Jukka O. Kauppinen. When asked about flying the Fw 190, Rall said:

> The 190, I had one ride in the 190—long nose. The 190 was a very stable aircraft. It had a very good weapons arrangement, you know they had two guns on top of the engine and two guns at the root of the wing. And a very stable undercarriage. It had a much better cockpit, a more comfortable cockpit. And it had a rotating engine. No problems with the cooling system with this type. Focke-Wulf was a good airplane and the long nose was even better for high altitude. But I cannot give you too [much] more. I flew it once, when I was in fighter leader school. By the way, the long nose came too late, anyway.

The Fw 190 A and F series rank among the best-looking radial fighter aircraft to emerge in the 1930s and 1940s. First impressions seem to be universal: observers find its lines and proportions very pleasing, with its large, blunt nose and wide-stance landing gear. The A-6 through A-8 best represent the type and comprise the bulk of total numbers of aircraft built. This series did the vast majority of the work during the war.

The Fw 190D was a better aircraft in most regards, but it came too late to change the course of the war. The long nose and extended fuselage gave it a distinctive appearance, but it perhaps lost some of the graceful lines of the radial-engine models.

Between sixteen thousand and twenty thousand Fw 190s were built, and it served on virtually every front attended by the Luftwaffe and its Axis allies. It was created in no fewer than forty variants and accounted for the destruction of a tremendous amount of Allied assets. This potent fighter's legacy is that it was one of the best ever to roam the skies.

LEFT: **Doras' Defense.** From 1944 to the end of the war the Luftwaffe operated in defense of the Reich. Most fighter units serving on the Eastern Front were pulled back to help defend Germany. JG 26, once one of the most successful frontline fighter groups on the Western Front, was kept busy in the skies over Germany, fighting a desperate battle against Allied aircraft intent on bombing Germany into submission.

Doras' Defense depicts Fw 190Ds of VII./JG 26 scrambling from their airfield in Nordhorn, Germany, in March 1945 to intercept an incoming formation of US bombers. The Fw 190D is considered by many not only one of the best fighter aircraft of World War II, but the best piston-engine fighter produced by Germany during the war.

FOCKE-WULF
Fw 190A

AIRCRAFT DEPICTED

Fw 190A-5

Flown by Hauptmann Walter Nowotny

I./JG 54

Russia

1943

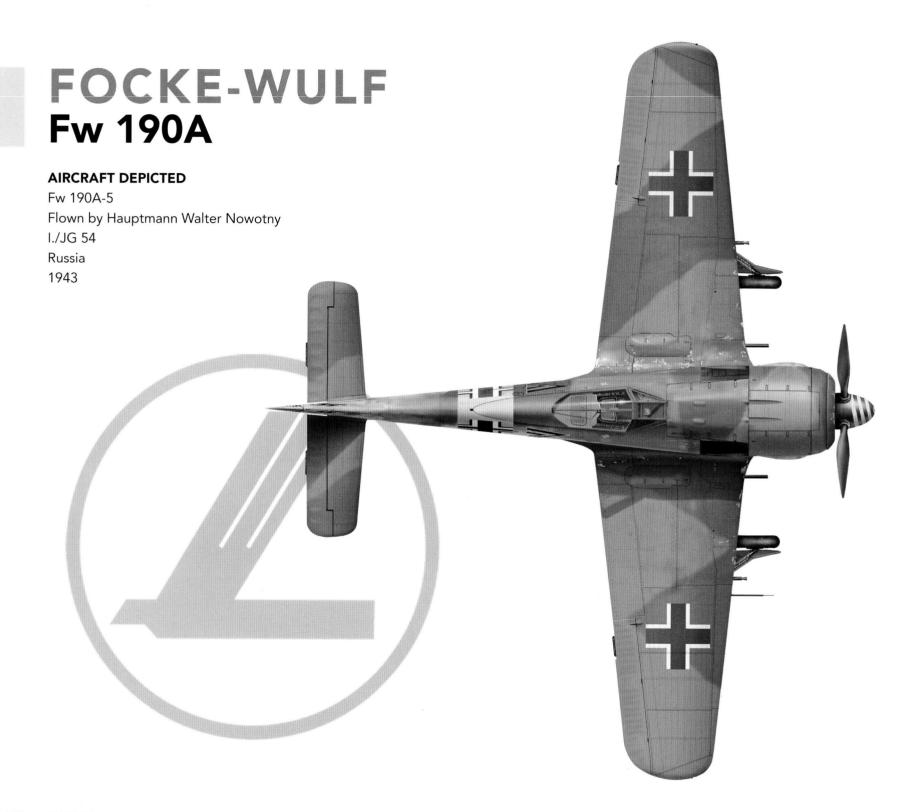

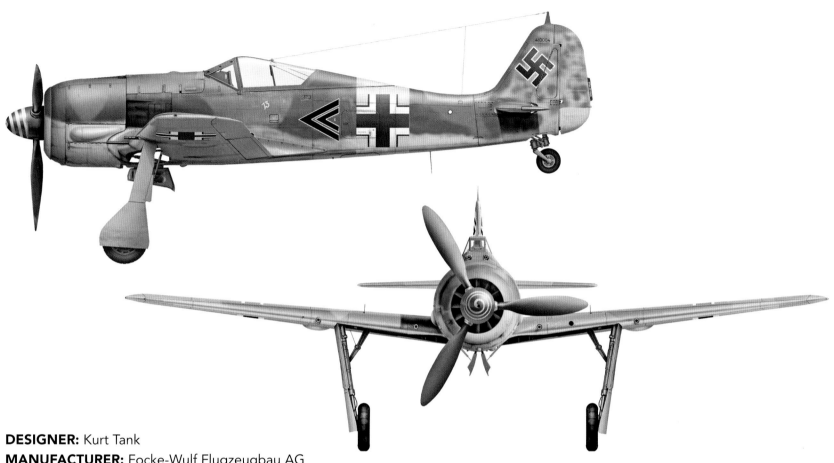

DESIGNER: Kurt Tank
MANUFACTURER: Focke-Wulf Flugzeugbau AG
AIRFRAMES PRODUCED: 16,000–17,000 estimated (including Ta-152)

SPECIFICATIONS

Length	29 ft 5 in (8.97m)	Maximum speed	392 mph (631kmh)
Wingspan	34 ft 5 in (10.49m)	Cruising speed	250 mph (402kmh)
Height	12 ft (3.66m)	Ceiling	33,600 ft (10,240m)
Empty weight	7,060 lb (3,202kg)	Range	741 mi (1,193km)
Loaded weight	9,480 lb (4,300kg)	Armament	20mm MG 151 cannons × 2
Engine	BMW 801D-2		MG FF 20mm wing-mounted cannons × 2
Output	1,770 hp		7.92mm MG 17 machine guns × 2
			(various gun packages used)

FOCKE-WULF
Fw 190D

AIRCRAFT DEPICTED

Fw 190D-9

Flown by Feldwebel Heinz Radlauer

13./JG 51, Mölders

Schmoldow, Germany

April 1945

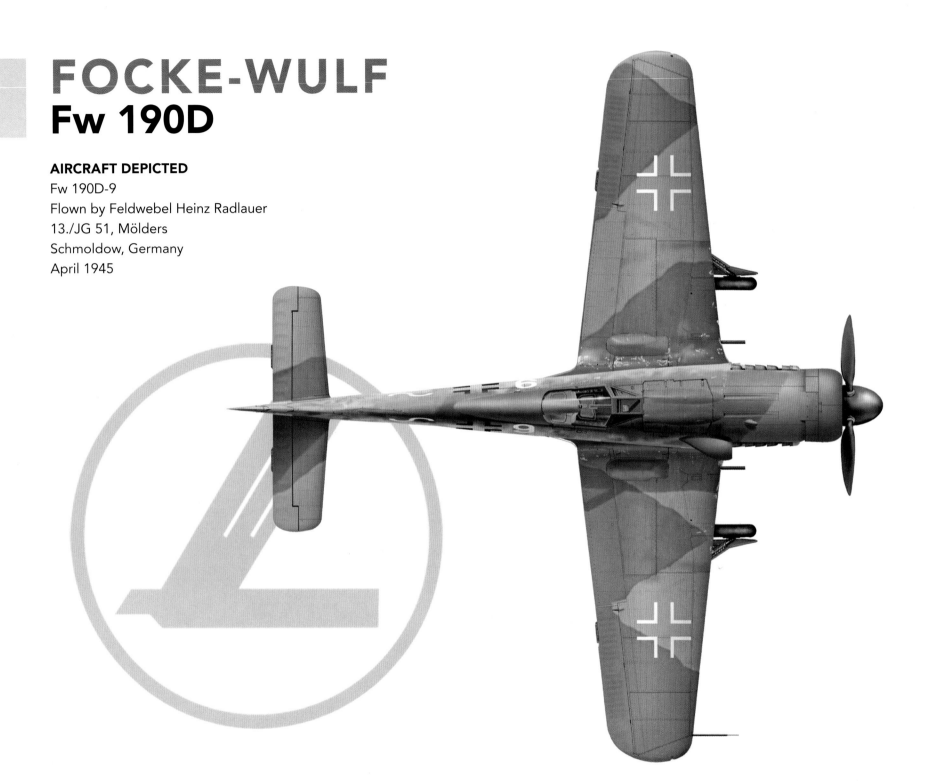

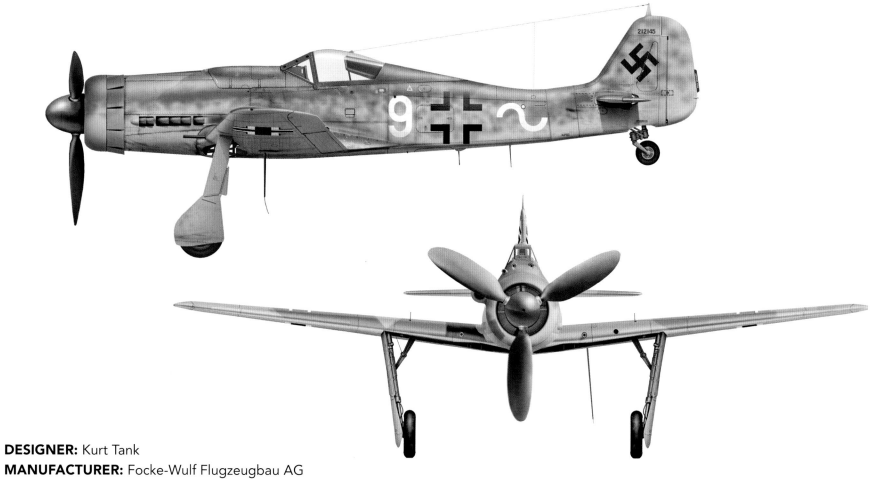

DESIGNER: Kurt Tank
MANUFACTURER: Focke-Wulf Flugzeugbau AG
AIRFRAMES PRODUCED: 674 (D models)

SPECIFICATIONS

Length . . . . 33 ft 5 in (10.19m)
Wingspan . . . . 34 ft 9 in (10.59m)
Height . . . . 11 ft (3.35m)
Empty weight . . . . 7,695 lb (3,490kg)
             (2,240 hp with water-methanol injection)
Loaded weight . . . . .9,480 lb (4,300kg)
Engine . . . . Junkers Jumo 213

Output . . . . 1,774 hp
Maximum speed . . . . 425 mph (684kmh)
Cruising speed . . . . 280 mph (450kmh)
Ceiling . . . . 39,400 ft (12,000m)
Range . . . . 518–598 mi (833–963km)
Armament . . . . 20mm MG 151 cannons × 2
                     13mm MG 131 machine gun × 1

FOCKE-WULF
Fw 190

1. FuG 16ZY communications and homing switch and volume control
2. FuG 16ZY receiver fine tuning
3. FuG 16ZY homing range switch
4. FuG 16ZY frequency selector switch
5. Tailplane trim switch
6. Undercarriage and landing flap actuation buttons
7. Undercarriage and landing flap position indicators
8. Throttle
9. Throttle-mounted propeller pitch control thumb switch
10. Tailplane trim indicator
11. Instrument panel lighting dimmer
12. Pilot's seat
13. Throttle friction knob
14. Column control
15. Rudder pedals
16. Wing gun firing button
17. Fuel tank selector lever
18. Engine starter brushes withdrawal button
19. Stopcock control lever
20. FuG 25a IFF control panel
21. Undercarriage manual lowering handle
22. Cockpit ventilation knob
23. Altimeter
24. Pilot tube heater light
25. MG 131 "armed" indicator lights
26. Ammunition counters
27. SZKK 4 armament switch and control panel
28. 30mm armor glass
29. Windscreen spray pipes
30. 50mm armor glass
31. REVI 16B reflector gunsight

32. Padded coaming
33. Gunsight padded mounting
34. AFN 2 homing indicator (FuG 16ZY)
35. Ultraviolet lights (port and starboard)
36. Turn and bank indicator
37. Airspeed indicator
38. Tachometer
39. Repeater compass
40. Clock
41. Manifold pressure gauge
42. Ventral stores and manual release
43. Fuel and oil pressure gauge
44. Oil temperature gauge
45. Windscreen washer operator lever
46. Fuel warning light
47. Engine ventilation flap control lever
48. Fuel contents gauge
49. Propeller pitch indicator
50. Rear fuel tank switchover light (white)
51. Fuel content warning light (red)
52. Fuel gauge selector switch
53. Propeller switch automatic/manual
54. Bomb fusing selector panel and external stores indicator lights
55. Oxygen flow indicator
56. Fresh air intake
57. Oxygen pressure gauge
58. Oxygen flow valve
59. Canopy actuator drive
60. Canopy jettison lever
61. Circuit breaker panel cover
62. Battery disconnect switch
63. Map holder
64. Operations information card
65. Flare box cover
66. Starter switch
67. Flare box cover plate release knob
68. Fuel pump circuit breakers
69. Compass deviation card
70. Circuit breaker panel cover
71. Armament circuit breakers

SUPERMARINE
Spitfire

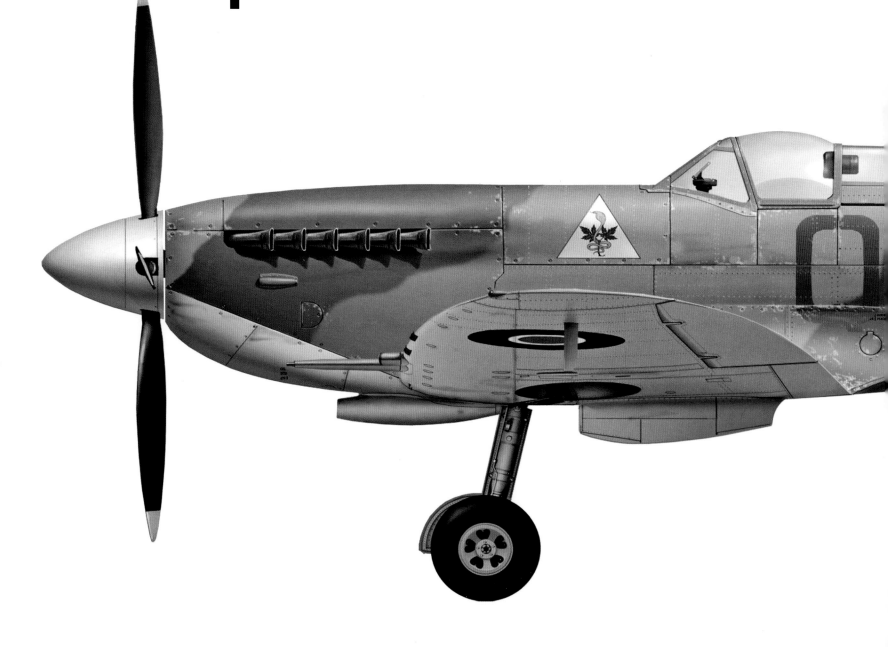

When the Battle of France ended in 1940, the defeated French and British forces pushed back across the English Channel, and the Germans prepared for the invasion of England. However, the Germans underestimated the resolve of the British and paid little heed to Winston Churchill's famous words, "We shall never surrender." One person in particular would play a key role in Germany's defeat.

Reginald J. Mitchell joined Supermarine Aviation Works, Ltd. in 1917 as an assistant designer, but was promoted to chief designer in 1920. Mitchell was a gifted artist with above-average mathematical ability, and over the next sixteen years he helped design twenty-four aircraft. One of his famous designs was the very advanced S4 seaplane racer, which won the Schneider Trophy in 1922. The race had dual purposes: promoting the advance of aviation technology with practical applications for the civil aircraft industry, and showcasing the latest aeronautical technology from each nation.

During the next few years, the Schneider Trophy passed from country to country as they leapfrogged one another with a sequence of rapid-fire advances in aircraft designs, thus fulfilling one of the race's goals. The early success of Mitchell's racing designs would pave the way for one of the most magnificent aircraft designs in history.

Despite Prime Minister Neville Chamberlain's nonaggression pact with Germany in 1938, Britain and other countries had been observing Hitler's aggressions in Europe since the early 1930s, and the possibility of war was becoming more apparent as the decade drew to a close. This plus the rapid buildup of German military assets compelled the British Air Ministry to seek designs for fighter aircraft. Specifications were issued in 1934 for an all-metal fighter with a top speed of 250 miles per hour (402kmh). R. J. Mitchell and his design team at Supermarine began work on the Type 224 interceptor, which would be powered by a Rolls-Royce Goshawk engine. The first example reached only 230 miles per hour (370kmh), but by then Mitchell had already begun work on its successor, the Type 300, which would look like the soon-to-become-legendary British fighter.

The first prototype to be called "Spitfire" was numbered K5054. It was powered by a newly designed Rolls-Royce PV-12 Merlin engine, had an enclosed cockpit and retractable landing gear, and carried two .303-inch machine guns in the wings. It was ready for its maiden flight on March 5, 1936, at Eastleigh, Southampton. Test pilot Joseph Summers reported that the airplane handled "beautifully." By this time the Air Ministry had revised its specifications to require fighters to carry eight .303 guns, so wing design modifications were among the first to be addressed going forward in the Spitfire's development.

Geoff Wellum. Squadron Leader Geoffrey Wellum served with RAF No. 92 Squadron during the Battle of Britain. On September 11, 1940, 92 Squadron was in one of many air battles defending Britain from the Luftwaffe. In this depiction, Wellum attacks Heinkel 111 bombers and Bf 109Es headed for the English coast; he would shoot down one of the bombers on this day.

PREVIOUS PAGES: Spitfire Mk. VII flown by Flight Lieutenant James Francis "Stocky" Edwards, RAF No. 92 Squadron, late 1943.

The Air Ministry was so impressed with initial flight tests that it ordered 310 machines to be built even before the official testing program was complete. The first Spitfire Mk I was put into service with No. 19 Squadron at RAF Duxford in August 1938. Improvements made to the Mk I included bulged canopy glass to improve visibility, armored front windshield glass, armor plating, and the newer Merlin Mk II engines mated to three-bladed, two-pitch propellers. Spitfire Mk IIs made their way into the fray in the summer of 1940, with even more powerful Merlin XII engines and more armor plating for pilot protection.

Supermarine began to experiment with various wing designs and armament using combinations of .303-inch guns and Hispano-Suiza 20-millimeter cannons. Wing designs were called A, B, C, or D depending on the gun packages used. Improvements continued, and the next variant, the Mk V, would become the most-produced type. A Mk V could be powered by a Merlin 45 or 46 engine and could carry external fuel tanks or bombs. As improvements continued, performance increased, and the Spitfire was pressed to serve a number of combat requirements. Heavier guns and the ability to carry bombs, for example, led to Spitfires operating in ground-attack and support roles.

The Mk V became the basis for other variants that were modified for different purposes. A lot of mixing and matching occurred at Supermarine, with different types cross-modified in various ways in experimentation or to suit particular uses. Mk VIs and VIIs had pressurized cockpits and extended wingtips fitted for high-altitude capability. Four-bladed Rotol propellers were fitted to various Merlin engine types. Fuel capacity was increased, the fuselage was strengthened internally, and a stronger wheel design was implemented. Some Spitfires had clipped wings for low-altitude duties.

As early as 1938, Supermarine had approached the British Admiralty with a proposal for a Spitfire designed for naval operations. It wasn't until early

1942 when a modified Mk V made its first carrier landing. Some modifications to the Seafire, as it was called, were the addition of arresting hooks and slinging points for launching. Early Seafires, however, suffered from structural weaknesses that made them unsuitable for the rigors of carrier landings. These problems were addressed in subsequent Seafire variants along with the addition of folding wings for storage. Rolls-Royce Griffon–powered Seafires were a bit tricky, as the engine's power gave the airplane a tendency to swing at full-power deck launches. The Seafire saw limited combat, with most produced in the latter half of the war. The last Seafire was taken out of service in 1954.

The Spitfire Mark IX was designed specifically to counter the Focke-Wulf Fw 190. The IX was the first variant to match the Luftwaffe fighter at higher altitudes, and it benefited from the use of the Merlin 63, 66, or 70 engine, which dramatically improved performance. In addition, it had the new Mk II gyro

ABOVE: This Supermarine Spitfire Mk VA was brought to the Langley Memorial Aeronautical Laboratory at Hampton, Virginia, for comparative testing in 1941.

OPPOSITE: *Battle over the Thames.* Flight Lieutenant Brian Carbury of No. 603 Squadron was one of the triple aces of the Battle of Britain. He was credited with fifteen solo aerial victories and another two shared, most of which were Bf 109 fighters, becoming the top-scoring Bf 109 killer of RAF Fighter Command during the Battle of Britain. On August 31, 1940, he downed three Bf 109s, including two in quick succession over the Thames estuary.

gunsight that made gunnery twice as accurate. Some late-production Mark IXs had a cut-down rear fuselage and a bubble canopy and could have clipped or standard wings fitted. Some of the changes and improvements to the Mark IX were used on other Spitfire variants.

As the design continually evolved, late-mark Spitfires had more competition from one another than from other aircraft types. New and more powerful Griffon engines with five-bladed Rotol propellers extended the Spitfire's capabilities in all tactical applications. Some of the Griffon-powered Spitfires reached altitudes of 44,000 feet (13,410m) and speeds of 443 miles per hour (713kmh).

The Mk XIV was a low-altitude version powered by Griffon 65 or 66 engines modified for low-altitude performance. For armament it carried two 20-millimeter cannons with either two .50-caliber or four .303-inch machine guns in the wings. One Mk XIV specialty was intercepting and destroying German V-1 flying bombs. The Mk XVI was similar to the XIV but was powered by a Packard-built Merlin. Most XVIs had clipped wings and bubble canopies.

The last Spitfire variant to serve in World War II was the Mk 21, armed with four 20-millimeter cannons. It arrived in April 1945 but saw little service. Marks 22 and 24 followed too late to see action. The Mk 24 made

Fox Hunt. On September 11, 1940, a II./ZG 76 crew, Feldwebel (literally, "Field Usher") Hermann Brinkmann and his radio operator, Unteroffizier (Sergeant) Erwin Grüschow, were over England when one engine of their Messerschmitt Bf 110C suddenly quit. They were immediately attacked by Spitfires, which damaged their other engine. They were headed for the English Channel but soon realized they wouldn't make it and began looking for a field to put down when they were attacked again. Brinkmann crash-landed in a field at Cobham Farm, Charing, and both men were made POWs.

ABOVE: Three USAAF pilots observe the performance of Spitfires firsthand.

RIGHT: Lieutenants E. D. Schofield of Belleville, Ohio, and R. F. Sargent of Youngstown, Ohio, prepare to pilot a British Spitfire. Under the Reciprocal Aid Program, Britain was furnished with critical American resources—including pilots.

its debut in the fall of 1946 and served in Malaya after the war.

Several foreign countries operated Spitfires before and/or after World War II: Australia, Belgium, Burma, Canada, Republic of China, Czechoslovakia, Denmark, Egypt, France, Greece, India, Indonesia, Ireland, Israel, Italy, Netherlands, New Zealand, Norway, Pakistan, Poland, Portugal, Southern Rhodesia, South Africa, the Soviet Union, Sweden, Syria, Thailand, Turkey, the United States, and Yugoslavia.

★ ★ ★

The Supermarine Spitfire is one of the most universally recognized and admired aircraft in the history of aviation. It had a graceful, elliptical wing design and a slim, curvy fuselage that made it look almost civil.

It was anything but. In the hands of a fighter pilot it became a deadly killing machine.

The Spitfire gained fame and legendary status during the Battle of Britain in 1940. Against superior numbers of Luftwaffe fighters and bombers, it dealt the Germans heavy losses. Along with the Hawker

Hurricanes, they were a key factor in saving Britain from invasion by Germany. The slower and stronger Hurricanes usually went after the bombers, while the faster and more maneuverable Spitfires typically dealt with the fighters.

The Spitfire's speed range was the widest of any fighter aircraft of World War II, with landing speeds as low as 65 miles per hour (105kmh) and top speeds nearing 450 miles per hour (724kmh). The Spitfire was the first Allied fighter to shoot down the new Messerschmitt Me 262 jet fighter, which could reach 540 miles per hour (869kmh). By all accounts, it was one of the easiest fighters to fly. Except for aileron forces in some situations, it required fairly light control inputs to execute maneuvers, and it was stable

in any flight attitude. Its remarkable performance and versatility were ample evidence of brilliant design.

More remarkable is the fact that this brilliance came from the mind of an aeronautical engineer with no formal training. Reginald "R. J." Mitchell had an inclination toward artistic design and mathematics. In 1917, when he was hired by Supermarine, he began as the owner's assistant, quickly learning whatever he could on the job while taking evening courses in engineering and math.

A great deal has been said and written about the Spitfire since its maiden flight in 1936. It is a highly coveted aircraft among war bird collectors, and a number of Spitfires still fly today, while still others are being restored to flying status.

The late author and pilot Jeffrey Ethell, who flew quite a few World War II fighters, wrote about the Spitfire Mk IX in *Air & Space Magazine* in 1995:

> Sitting behind this demon V-12 churning out so much power is intoxicating . . . the earth falls away at a rapid rate, at least for something with

a propeller. A look around reveals the excellent visibility out of the bubble canopy. This lessens, to a degree, the impression of being buried within a Spitfire, though that feeling of being a part of the machine does not change. . . .

> All Spitfires are exceptionally easy to land with no inherent tendency to swerve or ground loop. Just reduce power to idle, flare to a three-point attitude and she sets down on a feather almost every time. This is a great surprise to most considering the narrow track undercarriage and full swivel, non-locking tail wheel. Why doesn't it drop a wing violently or make the pilot stomp on the rudders? I wish I knew. The genius of managing to combine light aircraft characteristics with such high performance is nothing short of miraculous compared to most other wartime tail wheel types.

Invariably, any pilot who has experienced a flight in the Spitfire has walked away smiling. In his book *Fighter Pilot: The First American Ace of World War II*, Lt. Col. William R. Dunn of No. 71 Eagle Squadron wrote:

> The Spitfire was a thing of beauty to behold, in the air or on the ground, with the graceful lines of its slim fuselage, its elliptical wing and tail plane. It *looked* like a fighter, and it certainly proved to be just that in the fullest meaning of the term. It was an aircraft with a personality all of its own—docile at times, swift and deadly at others—a fighting machine "par excellence". . . .

> Once you've flown a Spitfire, it spoils you for all other fighters. Every other aircraft seems imperfect in one way or another.

On the other side, Luftwaffe pilots generally had a favorable opinion of the Spitfire as well. In a 1996 issue of *World War II* magazine, Colin Heaton

LEFT: Pilots from the RAF's 4th Fighter Group share a smoke in front of a Spitfire at Debden air base in North Essex, England.

RIGHT: **To Malta for Freedom.** In 1942, the British forces on the island fortress of Malta were under constant attack by the Luftwaffe. Prime Minister Winston Churchill concluded that the island faced invasion or surrender. In an attempt to bolster the position, US and British naval and air forces organized a joint effort called Operation Calendar. On April 20, 1942, the USS *Wasp* launched forty-seven Spitfires to Malta. All but one of them made it, greatly shoring up the island's defenses. Unfortunately, the following day, the Luftwaffe struck the island and destroyed all but seventeen of the Spitfires.

A second effort, Operation Bowery, used the aircraft carriers USS *Wasp* and HMS *Eagle*, with numerous support vessels filling out the carrier attack fleet. At dawn on May 9, 1942, a force of sixty-seven Spitfires departed the carriers for Malta; four were lost along the way. After landing on the island, the surviving Spits were immediately refueled and rearmed and met the Luftwaffe head on that day and the next, exacting a heavy toll on the Germans. This marked the turning point in the Battle for Malta. More Spitfires and Hurricanes arrived a week later, and from this island air base the British took control of Mediterranean shipping lanes, cutting off supply lines to Rommel's Afrika Korps. The Malta-based RAF sunk 70 percent of Italian and 23 percent of German merchant ships, changing the outcome of the war in North Africa.

In this image, RAF Sgt. L. Joseph Morsheimer (flying Spitfire Vc BR 169) and his squadron mates begin the 700-mile flight to Luqa Airdrome on Malta.

OPPOSITE: **Spitfire Supremacy.** In this imagined scene, mixed marks fly over the Belgian countryside after D-Day. A Spitfire Mk XII flies in the foreground while a Mk V and a Mk IX are seen in the background. Down below, a US armored vehicle unit passes a farm; one of the unit's officers has stopped to talk to the farmer regarding the knocked-out German Panther tank while the farmer's wife feeds the geese in the yard.

BELOW RIGHT: This formation of Spitfires was on intercept patrol over Djerba, off the coast of Tunisia, and on their way to the Mareth Line area.

BELOW: This Spitfire Mk VA was part of the USAAF's 555th Fighter Training Squadron, 496th Fighter Training Group at Goxhill, England, in 1944.

published his interview with Luftwaffe ace Günther Rall. "At the beginning of the war we flew short-range missions and encountered Spitfires, which were superior," Rall admitted. "I think that the Supermarine Spitfire was the most dangerous to us early on. I flew the Spitfire myself, and it was a very, very good aircraft. It was maneuverable and with good climbing potential."

Mitchell succumbed to cancer on June 11, 1937, at the age of forty-two, but lived just long enough to see the first flight of prototype K5054. In reading his biography, it seems he may have instinctively known that his fighter design was destined to become legendary. He was a unique individual in character and personality and, when it would have typically been the Air Ministry's position to dictate new aircraft designs, Mitchell's Spitfire was more the fulfillment of his dream than the result of meeting strict imposed specifications. Mitchell had no intention of letting authority constrict his imagination.

It is not known where Mitchell got his inspiration, but it seems as if he may have foreseen his destiny in life and followed its prescribed course, driven by some unseen force as he labored long hours and in pain from his cancer. R. J. Mitchell appeared for just the exact amount of time needed to bring to fruition an aircraft that helped change nothing less than the course of world history.

The Supermarine Spitfire was a masterpiece of aeronautical engineering that lives on today, inspiring spectators at air shows around the world and demonstrating what is possible through human imagination and determination. It is so sought after by aviation collectors that an industry has sprung up dedicated to restoring Spitfire aircraft and manufacturing parts for these Supermarine supermachines. Further, to this day the Spitfire remains one of the most beloved icons of British national pride.

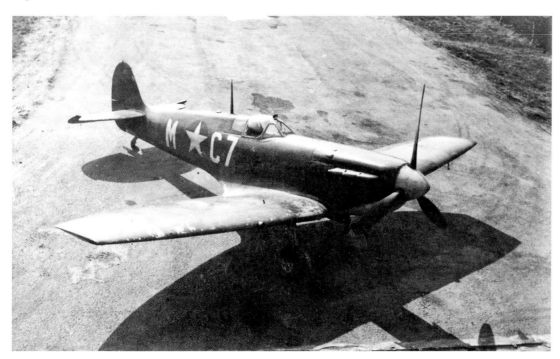

SUPERMARINE
Spitfire

AIRCRAFT DEPICTED

Spitfire Mk IIa

Flown by Flight Officer Geoffrey Wellum

No. 92 Squadron

Biggin Hill, Kent, England

1941

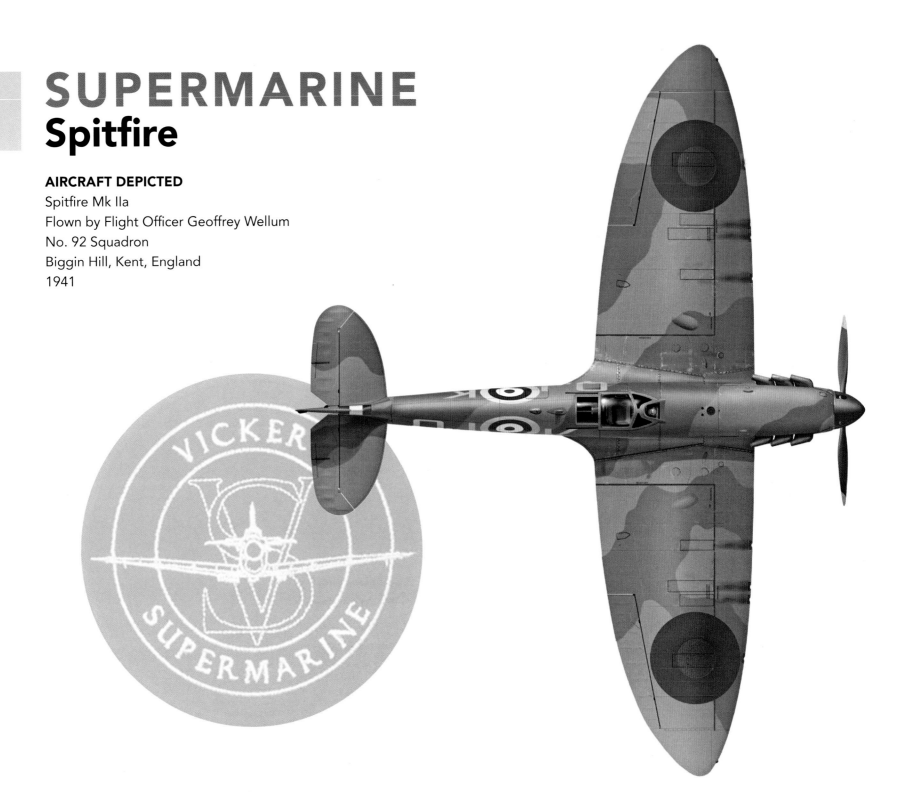

DESIGNER: Reginald J. Mitchell
MANUFACTURER: Supermarine
AIRFRAMES PRODUCED: 20,341

SPECIFICATIONS

Length . . . . 29 ft 11 in (9.12m)	Output . . . . 1,135 hp
Wingspan . . . . 36 ft 10 in (11.23m)	Maximum speed . . . . 354 mph (570kmh)
Height . . . . 9 ft 10 in (3.00m)	Cruising speed. . . . . 210 mph (338kmh)
Empty weight . . . . 4,541 lb (2,060kg)	Ceiling . . . . 37,000 ft (11,278m)
Loaded weight . . . . 6,172 lb (2,800kg)	Range . . . . .478 mi (769km)
Engine . . . . Rolls-Royce Merlin XII	Armament . . . . Browning .303-in machine guns × 8

SUPERMARINE
Spitfire

1. Boost control cutout
2. Brake triple-pressure gauge
3. Elevator tabs position indicator
4. Undercarriage tabs position indicator
5. Oxygen regulator
6. Flaps control
7. Blind flying instrument panel
8. Lifting ring for sunscreen
9. Reflector sight switch
10. Sunscreen
11. Gun and cannon three-position pushbutton
12. Cine-camera pushbutton
13. Reflector gunsight
14. Voltmeter
15. Ventilator control
16. Tachometer
17. Fuel pressure warning lamp
18. Boost pressure gauge
19. Oil pressure gauge
20. Oil temperature gauge
21. Radiator temperature gauge
22. Fuel contents gauge and pushbutton
23. Remote contactor and contactor switch
24. Slow-running cutout
25. Engine priming pump
26. Engine starting button
27. Booster coil pushbutton
28. Fuel cock control
29. Rudder pedal
30. Radiator flap control lever
31. Two-position door hatch
32. Cockpit floodlight
33. Camera indicator supply plug
34. Navigation lights switch

35. Control friction adjusters
36. Propeller speed control lever
37. Radio controller plug stowage
38. Elevator trimming tab handwheel
39. Camera-gun switch
40. Map case
41. Pressure head heater switch
42. Rudder trimming tab handwheel
43. Oil dilution pushbutton
44. Reflector sight lamps stowage
45. Signaling switch box
46. R.3002 pushbuttons
47. Harness release control
48. R.3002 master switch
49. CO_2 cylinder for undercarriage emergency system
50. Oxygen supply cock
51. Windscreen deicing pump
52. Windscreen deicing needle valve
53. Undercarriage emergency lowering control
54. Windscreen deicing cock
55. Tank jettison lever
56. Undercarriage control unit lever
57. Rudder pedal adjusting starwheel
58. Ignition switches
59. Signal discharger control
60. T.R. 1196 or T.R. 1304 controller
61. Fuel tank pressurizing cock control
62. Air-intake control (Seafire and Tropicalized Spitfire V only)
63. Throttle control
64. Pilot's seat
65. Oxygen hose
66. Airspeed indicator
67. Artificial horizon
68. Rate of climb indicator
69. Altimeter
70. Turn and slip indicator

CHAPTER 8

REPUBLIC P-47
Thunderbolt

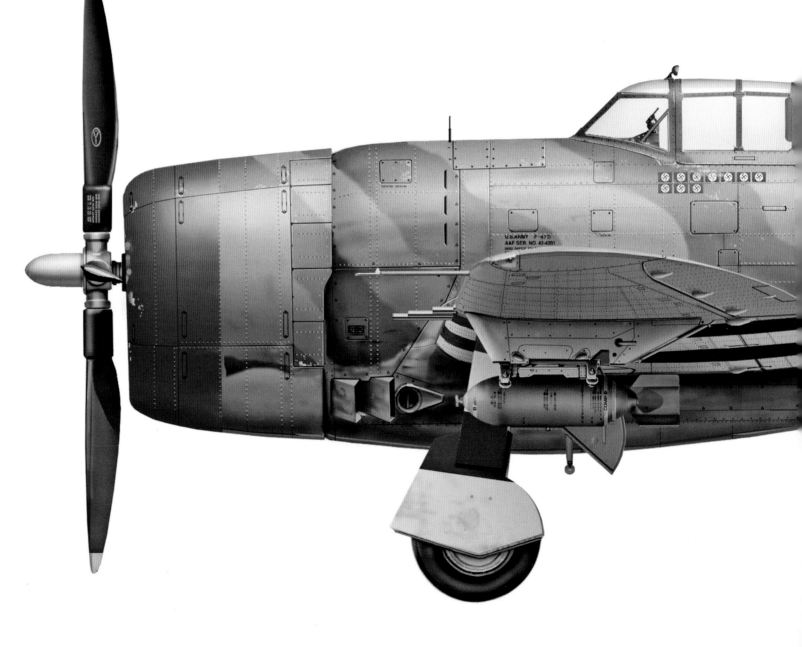

U.S. ARMY P-47D
AAF SER. NO. 42-4201

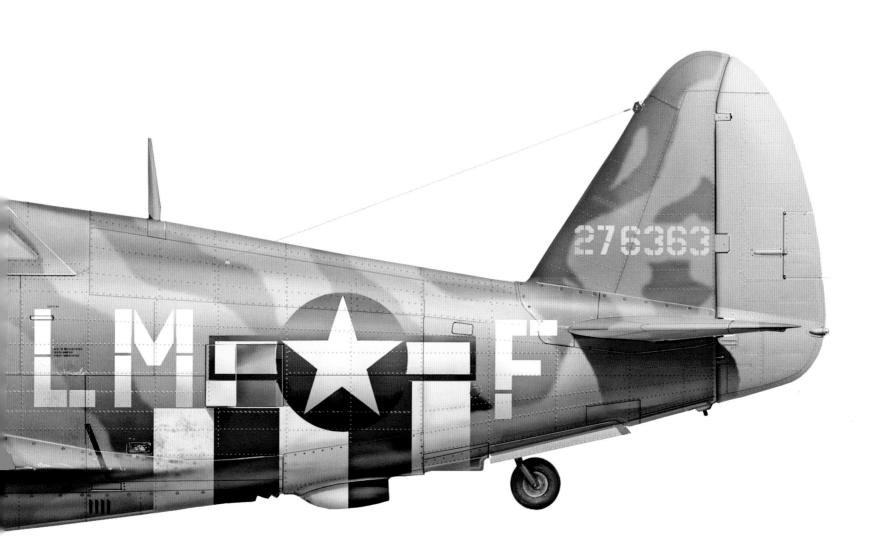

LM★F 276363

By the time the United States military complex found itself fully engaged in World War II, countries around the world had produced a flurry of new aircraft designs. And it soon became apparent to the US War Department that the European designs were far superior to any American aircraft currently in operation. New designs were urgently needed if the Americans were to at least keep pace with Axis counterparts.

The US Navy and US Army Air Corps had issued multiple contracts for various types of military aircraft. Stringent requirements were put on aircraft designers, often with a necessity to complete and test these new designs as quickly as possible. One such expedited contract resulted in what turned out to be one of World War II's most successful fighter designs: the Republic P-47 Thunderbolt. Although credit for the design went largely to an engineer named Alexander Kartveli, it was in fact the culmination of several years of collaboration between Kartveli and another ex-Russian, Alexander de Seversky. In his book *P-47 Thunderbolt in Action*, Larry Davis states that Seversky hired Kartveli in 1931 to join the Seversky Aircraft Corporation at Farmingdale, Long Island. "Kartveli was an engineering and aeronautical genius," Davis writes. "He already held patents on many extremely fast, industry standard–setting aircraft designs."

From 1933 to 1941 the Seversky-Kartveli team designed and refined a series of pursuit aircraft based on an all-metal, single-engined monoplane configuration beginning with the SEV-3 and culminating with the XP-43 and XP-44 designs. All these designs formed, in large part, the basis for what would become the P-47 design that excelled during the war.

In 1938, while Seversky was in Europe demonstrating the new EP1-68 fighter design, the Seversky Aviation Corporation board of directors elected a new president and reorganized the company under a new name: Republic Aviation Corporation. Alexander Kartveli, hired by Seversky in the early days, retained his position as vice president and would later expand on the designs he and Seversky had worked on together while developing the XP-43 and 44 series.

After Seversky's ouster in 1939, Republic continued with limited orders of the YP-43 and YP-44 while the "Arsenal of Democracy" semiquietly ramped up in anticipation of the war looming on the horizon. Sweden accounted for most of Republic's orders during this period, with a few small orders from China also helping to sustain the small company.

Eventually Materiel Command, compelled by rapidly changing and superior European designs, issued a new order to Republic Aircraft to develop a fighter aircraft with 2,000 horsepower, a top speed of 400 miles per hour (645kmh), and a service ceiling of 40,000 feet (12,200m). Kartveli wanted to use the brand-new

Mission Completed. The unmistakable black-and-white checkered noses of these P-47 Thunderbolts identify them as belonging to the 78th Fighter Group at Duxford, England. The 78th flew P47s and P-51s and accounted for 338 air-to-air and 358 air-to-ground victories during World War II. This is a semifictitious post-mission scene of a pilot being greeted in front of his P-47D "razorback." A ground crewman looks on with pride, knowing he has participated in the mission's success.

PREVIOUS PAGES: P-47D-22-RE Thunderbolt flown by 2nd Lt. Billy G. Edens, 56th Fighter Group, 62nd Fighter Squadron, August 1944.

turbocharged Pratt & Whitney R-2800 radial engine, and the army agreed when he promised to meet all their design requirements. The big radial engine, combined with an internal supercharging system, gave the new fighter its large fuselage. The new design was named the XP-47 and XP-47A.

The first of four preproduction models was tested at Republic's Farmingdale facility on May 6, 1941. Despite a few minor glitches, the test pilot declared the design a winner. Following refinements, further testing, and the loss of a couple of prototypes in accidents, the first true production model, the P-47B, was completed on May 26, 1942. The first of many P-47s was assigned to the 56th Fighter Group. The first in-theater group to receive the new P-47C was the 4th Fighter Group, made up of the Eagle Squadron pilots who had flown Spitfires in the Battle of Britain.

After its arrival in Europe, the P-47 continued to suffer some teething problems, all of which were resolved in due course (see below). Nonetheless, it performed adequately and proved a worthy adversary to the German Bf 109 and Fw 190. With its eight .50-caliber wing guns, the P-47 could saw through any aircraft—some gun camera footage shows wings and tail sections of German planes being ripped off from the concentrated fire of P-47s.

Davis writes, "The first encounter between the P-47 and the Luftwaffe occurred on 15 April (1943) when the 4th Fighter Group jumped some unwary Germans over France. Major Donald Blakeslee scored the first P-47 kill." It must have been a surprise to the Germans when they first saw this very large American fighter plane.

The first P-47D models arrived in the United Kingdom in April 1943, and the airplane found an important role in the European theater as a fighter-bomber, destroying all manner of ground targets. Among other ground-support missions, P-47s participated in the D-Day offensive supporting Allied troops and equipment as they landed on the beaches of Normandy and pushed toward the interior of Germany.

The P-47D would be the most-produced in the series, with 12,602 built. While the B and C models were used to dial in the Thunderbolt in combat, the shortcomings of these variants led to numerous improvements incorporated into the D series, beginning with the D-1 and ending in the D-40. In his book *Aircraft of the 8th AAF 1942–1945*, Kev Darling catalogs notable changes throughout the D series, including additional cowl flaps to help with cooling; improved engine systems such as oil, fuel, and hydraulics; bulletproof windscreen and improved pilot armor; a larger paddle propeller blade and a more efficient turbocharger; water injection for wartime emergency power; and a bubble canopy for better all-around vision. While it increased pilot visibility, the bubble canopy also eliminated the "razorback" spine aft of the cockpit, resulting in some yaw instability; a strake was added forward of the vertical stabilizer on the D-40 variant to counter this effect.

Affectionately nicknamed "Jug," the P-47 was one of the most famous fighter planes of World War II. Although originally conceived as a lightweight interceptor, it developed into a heavyweight fighter-bomber.

Neel Kearby. Lieutenant Colonel Neel E. Kearby of the 348th Fighter Group flew his last mission on March 5, 1944, to Wewak and a Japanese airfield at Dagua. From 22,000 feet, his group spotted a number of Japanese aircraft at about 1,000 feet, apparently preparing to land. The P-47s dove at high speed and tore into Japanese "Nell" and "Lily" bombers, downing several on the first pass. Within minutes, however, Ki-43 "Oscars" and Ki-61 "Tonys" came to the bombers' aid. All of the aircraft were in a swirling mass at low altitude when Kearby suddenly found an Oscar on his tail. He tried desperately to bank and climb as Capt. Bill Dunham made a head-on pass at the pursuing Oscar in an attempt to shake it off Kearby's tail. Dunham caught a brief glimpse of Kearby opening his canopy. He was apparently hit and may have been attempting to bail out or evacuate cockpit smoke.

In 1947 a Royal Australian Air Force search party found Kearby's wrecked P-47, *Fiery Ginger IV*, near Pibu, New Guinea, 140 miles away. Islanders found Kearby hanging from his parachute in a tree, already dead, and buried him. Kearby's remains were disinterred and returned to Dallas, Texas, where he was reburied at Hillcrest Memorial Park on July 23, 1949.

RIGHT: P-47 Thunderbolts from the 318th Fighter Group take off from East Field on Saipan, Marianas Islands, in October 1944. The lead ship, *Big Squaw*, is the Republic-Evansville P-47D-20-RA assigned to John "Jack" H. Payne of the 19th Fighter Squadron.

OPPOSITE: **Not My Turn to Die.** On June 26, 1943, Robert S. Johnson of the 56th Fighter Group was one in a flight of sixteen P-47 Thunderbolts assigned to escort B-24 bombers to their target. The P-47s were bounced from above by approximately sixteen Fw 190s. On the first pass, Johnson's plane was hit by 20-millimeter cannon rounds, and he found his canopy was jammed shut by the damage when he attempted to bail out. Though he was wounded and his airplane in bad shape, he realized he could still fly and set course for England. Nearing the coast of France, a lone Fw 190 spotted him and made numerous gunnery passes, firing cannons and machine guns. To the amazement of both men, the P-47 would not succumb. Finally, out of ammunition, the German pilot pulled in close to Johnson and looked over the battered Thunderbolt. Shaking his head in disbelief, he saluted Johnson and banked off toward his Luftwaffe base in France. Most historians believe the German was Luftwaffe ace Georg-Peter Eder of JG 2, who was ferrying a JG 26 aircraft on that day.

P-47D upgrades also included an increased internal fuel capacity to 375 US gallons (1,420L), as well as provisions to accommodate external fuel tanks and rocket rails. Steadily increasing fuel loads allowed P-47s to escort bombers all the way into Germany, something it was not able to do upon arrival in Europe.

And it wasn't only in Europe that the P-47 was showing its effectiveness. "By 1944 the P-47 was in combat with the USAAF in all its operational theaters except in Alaska where the Curtiss P-40 was preferred for the Battle of the Aleutian Islands," Darling writes. Elsewhere, the P-47 was used by other Allied countries to wreak havoc on Axis adversaries—foreign air forces using the P-47 in World War II included Russia, Brazil, Mexico, Britain, and France.

It is important to note one other fact about this robust fighter: The 56th Fighter Group was the first US group to receive the P-47 and the only group in the Eighth Air Force to use it throughout the war. "The

unit claimed 665.5 air victories and 311 ground kills, at the cost of 128 aircraft," Darling notes. "Despite being the sole remaining P-47 Group in the 8th Air Force, the 56th FG remained the top scoring group in aerial victories throughout the war."

The last two significant P-47 variants were the M and N models. Author Bill Gunston, in his book *The Illustrated Directory of Fighting Aircraft of World War II,* identifies the M as a "Sprint" version of the P-47 designed to chase V-1 flying bombs. It had six wing guns, wing air brakes, and an engine-turbocharger combination capable of producing 2,800 horsepower. The type was plagued with numerous problems, however, and saw very limited use. Only 133 examples were built.

The P-47N was much more successful version designed for high-altitude escort of B-29 bombers over Japan. Increased internal fuel capacity increased its range to 2,000 miles (3,200km). Its squared-off wingtips

OPPOSITE: **Wolf Pack Strikes.** In late February 1944, during the week known as "Big Week" to the Eighth Fighter Command, unusually clear weather afforded the Allies the opportunity to carry out massive bombing raids over much of Germany. The raids were met by large numbers of Luftwaffe fighters. P-47s, P-38s, and P-51s increased their victories substantially during this period.

The skilled P-47 Thunderbolt pilots of the 56th Fighter Group, known as "Zemke's Wolf Pack," enjoyed great success during Big Week. On February 24, three squadrons of the 56th were dispatched to escort bombing raids to Schweinfurt and other targets. Near Kassel, the 61st Squadron encountered Fw 190Ds. The squadron's CO, Maj. James C. Stewart, claimed one Fw 190 and one probable.

BELOW: This P-47D-22-RE was originally assigned to the 376th Fighter Squadron, 361st Fighter Group, and flown by Capt. John D. Duncan. The aircraft was later lost on August 3, 1944, while assigned to the 63rd Fighter Squadron, 56th Fighter Group, and flown by Lt. Roach Stewart Jr.

increased its roll rate, and it was fitted with a more powerful R-2800-77 engine.

After World War II, the P-47 remained in service with a number of foreign operators. In *P-47 Thunderbolt at War* Cory Graff notes that postwar Thunderbolts were used by France, Nationalist China, Portugal, Yugoslavia, Iran, Mexico, Turkey, Italy, Bolivia, Brazil, Chile, Colombia, Dominica, Ecuador, Guatemala, Honduras, Nicaragua, Peru, and Venezuela. "A handful of other Thunderbolts are rumored to have escaped official channels and ended up elsewhere—Haiti, Cuba, Communist China, and Argentina," Graff adds.

The overall service record of the Republic P-47 Thunderbolt, its ability to absorb tremendous punishment and bring its pilots home, and the various roles it played in combat cemented its reputation as one of the top-ten killer fighters of World War II.

★ ★ ★

Parked on a tarmac, a P-47 has all the characteristics of a bulldog: wide stance, thick chest and shoulders, and a block-shaped head. In the air, however, this fighter took on a much more streamlined look, with its beautiful elliptical wings and long fuselage tapering gently toward the tail and

its rounded tail planes. Both the early razorback and later bubble canopy designs are recognizable from any angle.

The Thunderbolt was the largest and heaviest single-seat fighter of World War II. When the first P-47s arrived at airbases in England, most were surprised at their size. Larry Davis wrote, "The new aircraft, designated XP-47B by the Army, was huge and did not appear streamlined at all. In fact, with its big, broad flat frontal area, and bulging under fuselage, it resembled a milk jug. So much so, that the name stuck —'JUG.' The British thought the name was short for 'Juggernaut'—a term in reference to both its size and firepower."

Officially, the XP-47 was called the Thunderbolt. But to those who flew and maintained them, they were always referred to as "Jugs." The cockpit was also large, especially compared to RAF and Luftwaffe fighters. Some British pilots commented that a P-47 pilot could simply get out of his seat and run around inside to evade enemy fire.

Though it was very large, the P-47's speed and maneuverability made it a lethal killing machine capable of tearing its enemies apart with eight .50-caliber machines guns, 5-inch rockets, or 500-pound bombs. It could take a great deal of punishment, too. In many instances P-47s returned safely, though completely riddled with holes from machine guns and cannon shells, sometimes with large parts of their wings and tail sections missing or even a complete engine cylinder blown off and most of the oil evacuated from the engine.

As with all new aircraft designs, the War Department put the Thunderbolt through extensive testing, recording in great detail every aspect of its performance at different altitudes, power settings, and more. Once in England, flight-comparison tests were conducted by Air Fighting Development Unit, RAF Station, Duxford, against all major fighter types then in use by the RAF. The comparison tests were aimed primarily at finding the best and worst attributes and using the data to train pilots on how to best use the new fighter in combat.

One area in which the Thunderbolt excelled was diving, due to its weight. This became a valuable asset, as no enemy aircraft could escape the P-47 by diving away, a tactic often used by Luftwaffe and Japanese pilots. A pilot could then use the energy from a dive to zoom back up to engage again, although he had to be mindful that, due its heavy weight, the energy would "bleed off" more quickly than it would with a lighter aircraft.

For the most part, the P-47 performed best at higher altitudes, which is what it was designed to do. Tests found the P-47 also had a very good roll rate, another advantage in aerial combat. In fact, the P-47N was found to have the best roll rate of the series with its squared-off wingtips. Last, but not least, was the withering firepower of eight Browning .50-caliber machine guns. With the addition of the K-14 computing gunsight, those guns became even deadlier.

When it flies by, the P-47 engine is not as loud as other big radial-engine planes, possibly owing to the fact that there isn't a cluster of short exhaust stacks sticking out from under the cowl flaps—just an exhaust flap on either side of the lower forward fuselage.

Pilots I spoke to said it was an easy aircraft to fly in all flight conditions. Control responses were straightforward, and it was easy to take off and land. The cockpit was comfortable, and instruments and controls were easy to reach. Visibility was very good, especially in models with the bubble canopy.

I have been fortunate to visit the homes of two of World War II's top Thunderbolt aces: Francis "Gabby" Gabreski (twenty-eight kills) and Robert S. Johnson (twenty-seven kills). Both reported that the Thunderbolt was a great-flying airplane with no significant vices. Both felt that it was the most survivable fighter aircraft of World War II in landing accidents and in combat, thanks to the sheer size and strength of the airframe.

I asked each what it was like when he fired the eight guns, and both said the fighter shook and almost felt like it slowed down from the recoil. A short, well-placed burst would mortally damage or outright destroy another aircraft. Both men agreed the firepower and durability of the P-47 gave its pilot a great sense of confidence.

ABOVE: Francis "Gabby" Gabreski scored twenty-eight kills in the Thunderbolt. He and Robert Johnson flew in the famed 56th Fighter Group, the only group to use the P-47 throughout the war.

OPPOSITE: *Calm Before the Storm.* The 56th Fighter Group was the only unit to fly the P-47 Thunderbolt through the entire war. Led by Col. Hubert "Hub" Zemke, they were known as Zemke's Wolfpack. These P-47s are depicted in post-D-Day livery at Boxted, England, as ground personnel prepare the aircraft for the day's first sortie. No fighter plane would ever have lifted into the sky for battle if not for the efforts of the ground crew, who worked tirelessly in all conditions to keep as many aircraft serviceable as possible. Every pilot holds these men in high regard. When this image first appeared in a magazine in 1994, Zemke wrote a letter to me stating it was the best artist image he had seen depicting his group and made the offer to sign all prints if I made them. Francis "Gabby" Gabreski agreed to do the same, and this became my first pilot-signed limited-edition print.

LEFT: This P-47D belonged to the 19th Fighter Squadron, 318th Fighter Group, and is seen here in Saipan. The D variant would go on to become the most-produced version of the Thunderbolt.

ABOVE: Robert S. Johnson was one of the top P-47 aces with twenty-seven kills. He reported that the Thunderbolt was a great-flying airplane with no significant vices.

RIGHT: A 37th Fighter Squadron Republic F-47N-25-RE over Dow Air Force Base, Maine, in 1948. This aircraft was part of the final Thunderbolt production at Farmingdale, New York.

OPPOSITE: **Red-E-Ruth.** *Red-E-Ruth* was a P-47N Thunderbolt piloted by Lt. Leon Cox of the 19th Fighter Squadron, 318th Fighter Group, based on Ie Shima in 1945. The 318th flew mainly ground-support missions with the US Marines and was the first fighter unit to use napalm in ground-attack missions. This image is a depiction of P-47s of the 318th attacking a Japanese airfield somewhere in the Japanese islands in the summer of 1945. Cox is attempting to avoid antiaircraft fire after pulling up from his first attack on the airfield. The P-47N could carry more fuel in its wings, and with drop tanks it had a range of 1,425 miles (2,300km), making it possible to hit distant targets. It could also be equipped with ten 5-inch High Velocity Aircraft Rockets (HVARs). Pilots claimed it could carry its own weight in fuel and ordnance.

When I visited Johnson at his home in Lake Wylie, South Carolina, he recounted what has become one of the most famous air combat incidents of the war when, on June 26, 1943, he nearly lost his life on his first bomber escort mission. This story became well known when Martin Caidin and Johnson cowrote the book *Thunderbolt!* in 1958. Johnson's flight was bounced by a group of Fw 190s, and he was knocked down and out of control by 20-millimeter cannons. Unable to bail out due to damage to the rear of the canopy, he regained control of his aircraft, only to be attacked three times by another Fw 190 over France. The German fighter had only 7.92-millimeter ammunition on board, but every last round was expended on Johnson's P-47 at close range. Failing to down the American, the Luftwaffe pilot saluted Johnson and peeled off just before they reached the English Channel.

In 1994, I spent four days at Gabreski's home not far from the former Republic Field on Long Island, New York. We had many chats about fighting the Germans and flying the P-47. Both Johnson and Gabreski flew in the famed 56th Fighter Group, the only group to use the Thunderbolt throughout the war. While most other units transitioned to the P-51, pilots like Johnson and Gabreski used their big fighters with great success, as did many other pilots in the 56th.

When I left, Gabreski gave me a gift: raw gun camera footage given to him by a famous Luftwaffe ace. Though it was all in German, the footage showed in stark black and white many one-on-one combats against P-47s, leaving no questions as to the Thunderbolt's abilities. Despite all the technical data from flight testing, unfavorable opinions of the P-47 from pilots of other types, and endless chatter on the Internet from the inexperienced and the uninformed, that film proves the Luftwaffe had a very hard time fighting the P-47. Time and time again, skilled pilots are outflown by the big, fat Thunderbolt.

There always has been, and always will be, much debate on which World War II fighter was the best. Opinions number nearly as many as wartime aircraft production numbers, but the facts speak for themselves. The overall combat record of the P-47 Thunderbolt leaves little room for debate. Its innovative design had a special purpose, it met or surpassed all its design requirements, and it served beyond expectations in every theater. It simply was one of the best aircraft of World War II.

REPUBLIC P-47
Thunderbolt

AIRCRAFT DEPICTED

P-47D-28-RE Thunderbolt, *Live Bait*
Flown by Captain Clayton Gross
355th Fighter Squadron, 354th Fighter Group
December 1944

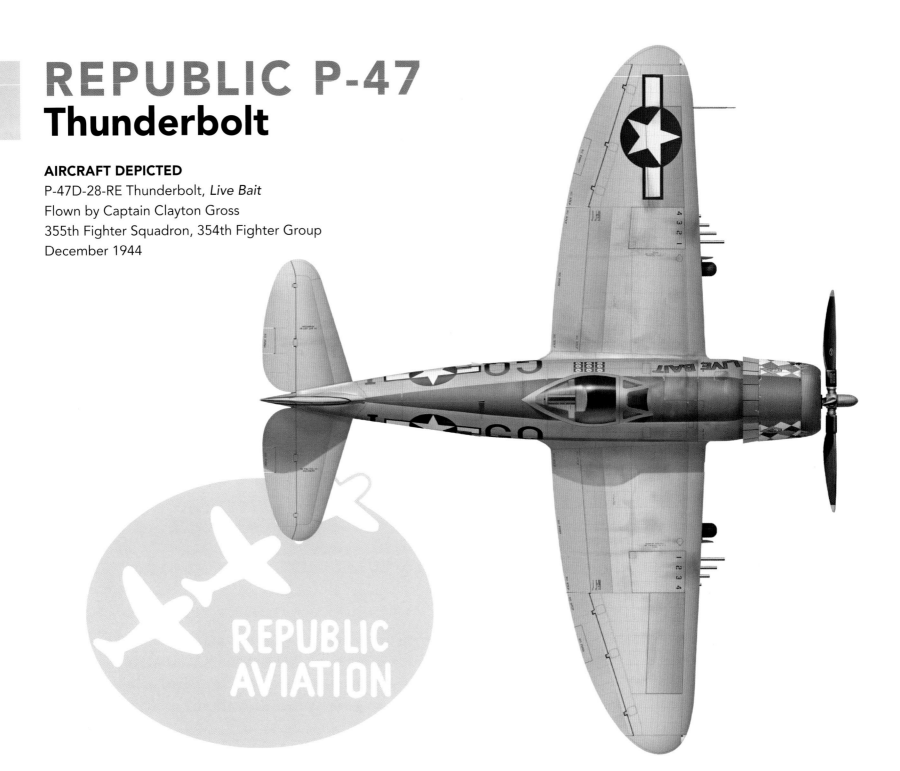

REPUBLIC
AVIATION

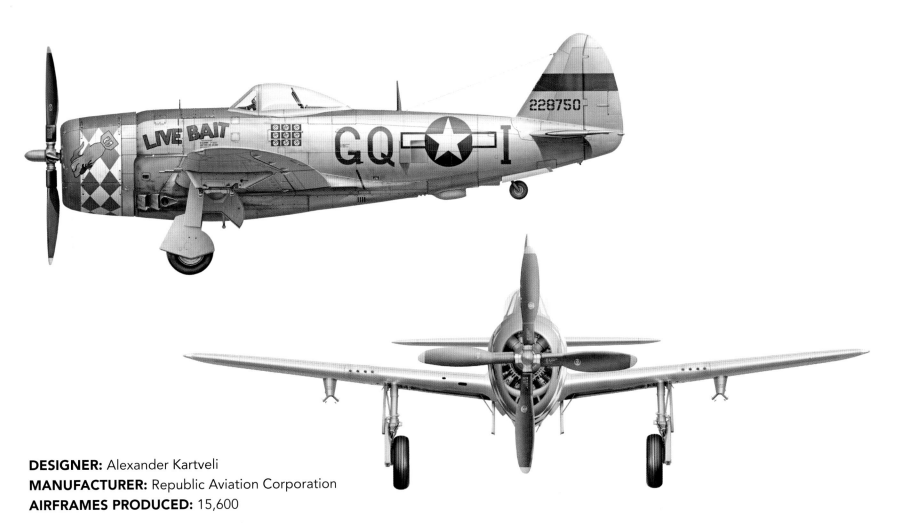

DESIGNER: Alexander Kartveli
MANUFACTURER: Republic Aviation Corporation
AIRFRAMES PRODUCED: 15,600

SPECIFICATIONS

Length . . . . 36 ft 1.75 in (10.71m)
Wingspan. . . . . 40 ft 9.75 in (12.44m)
Height . . . . 14 ft 7 in (4.45m)
Empty weight. . . . . .9,500 lb (4,309kg)
Loaded weight. . . . . .17,000 lb (7,711kg)
Engine . . . . .Pratt & Whitney R-2800-63
Output. . . . . 2,800 hp

Maximum speed . . . . 428 mph (690kmh)
Cruising speed. . . . . 260 mph (418kmh)
Landing speed. . . . . 99 mph (160kmh)
Ceiling . . . . 41,000 ft (12,500m)
Range . . . . .1,700 mi (2,735km) maximum
Armament . . . . .50-caliber machine guns × 8
2,500 lb (1,134kg) bombs

REPUBLIC P-47
Thunderbolt

1. Landing gear control lever
2. Elevator trim tab control wheel
3. Carburetor hot-air lever
4. Fuel level light
5. Rudder trim tab control
6. Aileron trim tab control
7. Cowl flap control
8. Cockpit light switch
9. Mixture control lever
10. Throttle quadrant locks
11. Throttle lever
12. Propeller control lever
13. Supercharger control
14. Cockpit light
15. K-14A gunsight
16. Clock
17. Artificial horizon
18. Airspeed indicator
19. Turn and bank indicator
20. Tachometer
21. Altimeter
22. Vertical-speed indicator
23. Carburetor air temperature gauge
24. Cylinder-head temperature gauge
25. Oxygen-flow blinker
26. Oxygen pressure gauge
27. Ignition switch
28. Master battery switch
29. Turbo tachometer
30. Compass

31. Oil temperature and pressure gauge
32. Hydraulic pressure gauge
33. Fuel quantity gauge
34. Directional gyro turn indicator
35. Suction gauge
36. Clock
37. Manifold pressure gauge
38. Battery amps gauge
39. Flare gun port
40. Engine primer
41. Oxygen hose
42. Oxygen regulator
43. Cockpit lights control
44. Fuel selector valve
45. IFF radio destroyer buttons
46. Identification lights switch
47. Command transmitter box
48. Command receiver control box
49. Cockpit vent control
50. Crystal filter selector button
51. Rudder pedals
52. Control column
53. Pilot's seat
54. Circuit breakers
55. Flare gun storage
56. Main circuit breakers
57. Main switch box
58. Gun safety switch
59. Parking brake handle
60. Flaps control lever
61. Recognition lights controls

CHAPTER 9

NORTH AMERICAN
P-51 Mustang

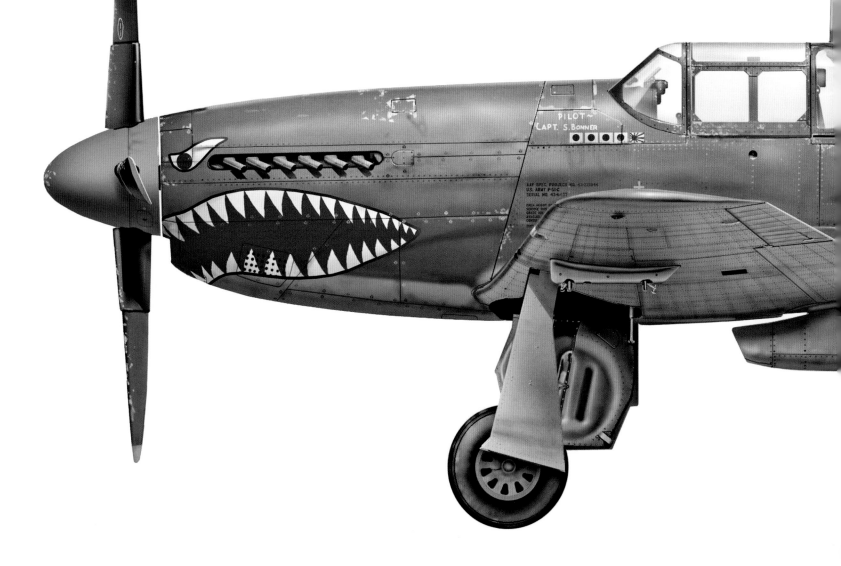

The old adage "necessity is the mother of invention" was never more pertinent than in World War II. With conflict raging across the Pacific and Atlantic Oceans, the United States sat smack in the middle of it all while trying to maintain its pacifist position. Meanwhile, the warring nations abroad were busy producing new weapons of all kinds, many of them well ahead of what the United States had in its inventory.

The volume of war materiel strained the production capabilities of every country, especially the smaller ones with limited resources. Great Britain was feeling this strain in 1940 as Germany tried to conquer it by air, on land, and at sea.

Attacking Britain from the sea has never been easy, so Germany decided the best strategy was to attack British shipping, then soften up Britain with sustained aerial bombing, which the Germans hoped would pave the way for a land assault.

The British fought around the clock to repel the Luftwaffe, which was relentless in its bombing attacks. The RAF had fewer aircraft in inventory than did the Germans, and RAF pilots and machines were pushed to their limits. They were desperate and turned to the United States for help. Most immediately, they needed more fighter aircraft.

In his book *P-51 Mustang*, Robert Grinsell wrote, "The British government sent a delegation of aircraft officials (under the auspices of the British Air Ministry) to the United States, which at that time had not entered the war or made any commitments to the war effort. The delegation was to survey the American aircraft fabrication potential in the hopes of augmenting the aircraft industry of the Commonwealth."

When the British Purchasing Commission arrived to survey American fighter aircraft, they were shown two fighters: the Curtiss P-40 and the Bell P-39. Though the P-40 was not the optimum choice for the RAF, it was chosen over the P-39 because it seemed to be the better choice for their purposes, but also there were no other better designs available. North American Aviation (NAA) was already producing NA-16 trainers for the British, who asked NAA if they could license-build P-40s for them because Curtiss was at full production capacity. NAA told the British they could build P-40s but would need about 120 days to set up tooling.

The president of NAA, noting the British had reservations about the P-40, suggested a new fighter design would be possible that would surpass the performance of the P-40. The British had a good business relationship with NAA, and with little more than trust accepted the proposal with the stipulation that the new design be completed within 120 days.

George Preddy's Last Chase. George Preddy was World War II's highest-scoring Mustang ace, with twenty-eight victories. On one mission in 1944, he scored six kills in the span of a few minutes. Preddy was a natural fighter pilot; usually quiet and always aggressive, he didn't mind "mixing it up" in the air or on the ground. Well regarded by all who knew him, Preddy was dealt a sad fate on Christmas Day 1944, when he was accidentally shot down by US antiaircraft units in Germany as he chased a low-flying Fw 190. American gunners were jumpy when they heard the sound of approaching aircraft engines. At the first sight of aircraft, they opened fire, ironically missing the German plane and hitting both Mustangs.

PREVIOUS PAGES: P-51B-7-NA Mustang flown by Capt. Stephen J. Bonner, 23rd Fighter Group, 76th Fighter Squadron, June 1944.

North American designers and engineers set themselves to the task of creating the new fighter plane using a design method called "lofting"—using mathematical tables to create objects with compound curves and advanced, streamlined features. The P-51 Mustang was one of the first modern aircraft designed by this method in the precomputer era.

The new design was designated the NA-73X and was powered by the Allison V-1710-39 twelve-cylinder engine. The first prototype was completed in 102 days without the engine. The engine was installed, and on October 26, 1940, the first example, serial number NX1998, made its maiden flight. Performance was impressive, and the British ordered 320 aircraft, which they called the "Mustang." They named them the Mustang I, II, III, and IV as the type evolved. NAA called the new design the XP-51 during its prototype and evaluation phase and then the A, B, C, and D models during regular production. The first new fighters used by the US Army Air Forces were named the P-51A Mustang; a dive-bombing variant called the A-36 Apache had dive brakes above and beneath the wings.

One feature that made the Mustang so successful was its advanced airfoil design. The P-51 utilized a new "laminar flow" airfoil designed by the National Advisory Committee for Aeronautics in 1940. The design depended on absolute tolerances and perfectly smooth surfaces to ensure no interruption of airflow over the wing. The design also featured a maximum chord thickness area that was located 40 percent rearward from the leading edge of the wing and was almost symmetrical in profile top to bottom. All this created very little drag effect on the Mustang wings and made it extremely "slippery" aerodynamically.

Possibly the greatest design advancement for the Mustang resulted from the installation of the Rolls-Royce Merlin engine. The British received their first Allison-powered Mustangs in the spring of 1942 and were very enthusiastic about them, although they did not perform as desired at very high altitudes. Plans were

made to refit the Mustangs with Rolls-Royce engines. The first marriage of the Rolls-Royce Merlin to a Mustang occurred in the summer of 1942, accompanied by numerous other design modifications, including strengthened engine mounts, relocation of a smaller front air scoop, a deepened and improved underbelly radiator with a more streamlined intake scoop, and a new four-bladed propeller with a radius of 11.4 feet (3.5m). The result was a more powerful, sleeker Mustang that could reach 432 miles per hour (695kmh) at 22,000 feet (6,705m).

The first Mustang Is had two .30-caliber and one .50-caliber machine guns in each wing. Mustang IIs had four wing-mounted .50-caliber guns. The airplane's long-range capabilities were realized immediately, and the RAF modified some Mustangs for long-range photo recon missions. On July 27, 1942, the Mustang became the first Allied fighter to fly into Germany, attacking targets in the Ruhr region.

An experimental North American XP-51, the second built, photographed in late December 1941. This version had a birdcage canopy, a three-bladed propeller, and an Allison engine.

From this point on, orders for Mustang from the USAAF and RAF increased at such a rate that the North American Aviation plant in Los Angeles could not keep pace, so North American pressed a subsidiary plant in Dallas, Texas, into service. The new Merlin-powered P-51s being built in Los Angeles were designated P-51Bs, while those in Dallas were P-51Cs (the two being virtually identical, which is why production models were typically referred to as P-51B/Cs). Subsequent production runs of the D models built in California and Texas were called P-51D NA and NT, respectively.

The first Allied fighter unit to receive the new P-51B/C was the newly formed 354th Fighter Group based at Boxted, England. The Mustangs arrived in November 1943 and flew their first combat missions into Germany three weeks later. On the first few missions the Luftwaffe offered no opposition; when the first Luftwaffe fighters, Bf 110s, finally saw the Mustang, they turned and ran, suggesting that the Mustang's reputation had preceded its arrival in Europe. The 354th Fighter Group would go on to destroy more than seven hundred enemy aircraft in air-to-air combat, more than any other Allied combat group in the war.

P-51 B/C models, which served in every combat theater of World War II, had a high dorsal spine fuselage profile and were equipped with two .50-caliber machine guns in each wing. The canopy was a hinged "birdcage" style with small quarter windows on each side of the aft canopy area to give the pilot a rear view over his shoulder. One early modification made by the RAF to its Mustang IIIs was replacing the standard canopy with a "Malcolm hood" featuring a bubbled

A P-51 Mustang is tested in the Full-Scale Tunnel at Langley Memorial Aeronautical Laboratory.

one-piece main canopy glass that provided a better view and slid rearward rather than being hinged.

Design modifications continued throughout Mustang production. The next big changes came with the introduction of the D series, which featured six .50-caliber wing-mounted machine guns, a bubble canopy, a more powerful engine, and increased fuel capacity to further extend its range. Underwing hard points were strengthened to accommodate larger drop tanks or 1000-pound bombs. Some D models could carry 5-inch rockets under the wings as well. With the six machines came an increase in the number of rounds that could be carried, a bit more than was necessary for the six guns. The new bubble canopy allowed the aft dorsal fuselage to be lowered, a modification that created some stability problems eliminated by fin fillets installed forward of the vertical stabilizer.

More P-51Ds were built than all other variants combined, but some other notable versions were produced, too. The P-51H was designed as a lightweight high-altitude interceptor with a high rate of climb. Davis states in *P-51 Mustang in Action*, "The P-51H was basically an XP-51F with a thirteen inch stretch to the fuselage using the Packard V-1650-9 which delivered 1,380 horsepower at 3,000 rpm and 2,270 horsepower in War Emergency Low Blower setting with water injection." Test flights proved a top speed of 466 miles per hour (750kmh) at 29,000 feet (8,840m) and a rate of climb of 4,000 feet (1,220m) per minute. A few other engines were tested with favorable results, but by the time the H was in production, the war was coming to an end, and the model never saw combat.

The P-51K was basically a D model with a few modifications, including a slightly higher-profile canopy for more headroom and a hollow steel-blade Aeroproducts propeller. A number of D and K models were configured as photo-recon ships (called the F-6), which carried three cameras for low-, medium-, and high-altitude photography, as well as six wing-mounted machine guns.

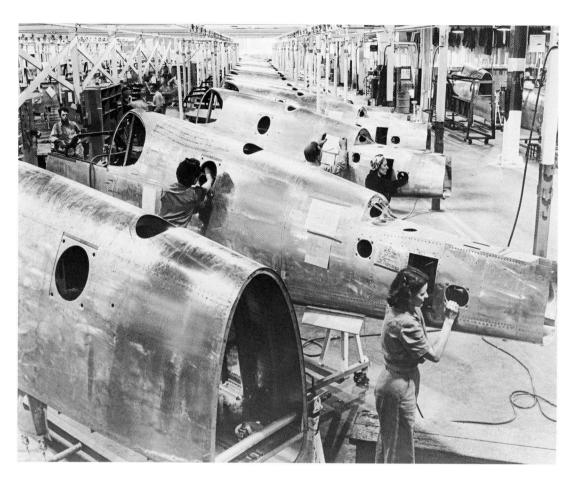

The P-82/F-82 Twin Mustang was the last, and oddest, rendition of the P-51. Conceived as a very long-range bomber escort for missions to Japan, it featured two Packard V1650-11/21 engines delivering 2,270 horsepower each with water injection, counter-rotating propellers, a lengthened rear fuselage, a range of 2,000 miles (3,220km), and two cockpits (only one with a complete set of instruments). Pylons under the wings held drop tanks and/or napalm, and the C through H variants were equipped with search radar pods that required one of the cockpits to be manned by a pilot/radar operator. Some of the radar Mustangs were painted gloss black for night operations. Later models could also carry various weapons and ordnance loads like gun pods, bombs, and rockets.

The amount of retooling and mobilization required to repurpose the US aviation industry for wartime production was staggering. This shot depicts North American Aviation's production line for P-51 fuselage.

Wooden wheels are attached to a P-51 so it can be moved around the ramp at North American Aviation's Inglewood, California, plant in 1942.

Overall, the twin Mustangs were great performers and versatile enough to be used in a variety of roles. None of them were completed in time to be used in World War II, but they did see service a few years later in Korea. The F-82 Twin Mustangs remained in service until mid-1951, when they were phased out by the arrival of new jet fighters.

The Mustang was easily one of the world's most widely used fighter aircraft. Different variants of the P-51/F-51 Mustang saw service with numerous other countries up until the early 1960s, including: Great Britain, Australia, New Zealand, Canada, Korea, the Netherlands (East Indies Air Force), Indonesia, Soviet Union, China, Sweden, Israel, Italy, Switzerland, South Africa, Philippines, Cuba, Dominican Republic, Haiti, Guatemala, Bolivia, Uruguay, Venezuela, El Salvador, Nicaragua, and Costa Rica.

★ ★ ★

The Mustang's history, from conception to the last one built, suggests a nearly perfect machine, as if fate was on its side before the plans were even drawn. To my mind, there has never been, and never will be, another fighter plane like the P-51 Mustang. It is one World War II's fighter planes that I can talk about from personal experience, having had the opportunity to fly two examples.

When I realized I was going to fly a P-51 for the first time, having never dreamed I would ever have the chance to do so, I could barely control my emotions. I was a private pilot with only sixty hours recorded in my flight log. I wouldn't be flying alone, as it isn't easy to transition from small civilian airplanes to high-powered military aircraft without a good deal of instruction time. I would be flying a 1945 P-51D Mustang converted to a tandem-seat fighter trainer known as the TF-51. My instructor was a Vietnam veteran with 103 combat missions to his credit.

Walking up to the Mustang for the first time, I immediately sensed something special about it. It is one of the few aircraft that look good from absolutely every conceivable angle, whether on the ground or in the air. It looks like a sleek, predatory cat—not brutish, like a lion or a tiger, but more like a cheetah or panther. How did men create such a machine so long ago and in such a short time? It is a timeless design that looks as good today as it must have looked to young pilots in the early 1940s.

I was given a preflight briefing covering the basic performance data of the aircraft and what kind of maneuvers would be performed. I wanted to do everything the plane was capable of, right up to the edge of its flight performance envelope, knowing I would probably make myself sick (which I did)—but I didn't want to deny myself the full experience of really flying it, just short of a live-ammunition firing pass on a target.

After the preflight inspection, with me listening to every word the pilot said while trying to take in every detail of the machine, it was time to climb in and buckle up the chute and seat harnesses, with the pilot relaying last-minute information to me the whole time—how

to unbuckle and bail out in an emergency, stall recovery, and other verbal notes on the instruments and controls. As I got into my seat, I was impressed by the cockpit's layout, which indicated the amount of thought given by its perfectionist designer.

I asked to taxi out and take off, but was told not the first time, as that could get the uninitiated into some trouble quickly. With the prestartup check list complete, the pilot shouted, "Clear prop!" and turned the prop over about five or six blades (the number of times a propeller blade passes by the pilot's forward view over the nose before the magnetos are turned on). The big Merlin coughed to life with a puff of smoke, then settled into a raspy purr. Already I was experiencing things no film can convey: the smells of exhaust, radiator coolant, hydraulic fluid, plastics, and metals. The plane rocked gently from the prop washing over the fuselage, and I became aware of the power sitting up in front of me in the cowling. This was no Cessna or Piper. This was a really powerful machine that demanded respect. And like its namesake, the Mustang, it would be very unforgiving if it was mishandled or disrepected.

Because there is no forward view over the nose, taxiing to the runway required S turns to the left and right to keep a view in front. Short of the runway, we performed an engine run-up and final check: oil pressure, cylinder temperature, propeller pitch controls, magneto checks, controls free and moveable. All good and ready to go, the big moment had arrived.

After final clearance to take the active runway, we taxied onto the threshold and rolled forward for a few feet to get the tail wheel tracking in a straight line, then pulled all the way back on the stick to lock the tail wheel into position.

We set the rudder and elevator trim tabs for takeoff, set propeller pitch, and slowly eased the throttle forward to 3,000 rpm. The Mustang quickly gained speed down the runway. We were at 60 to 70 miles per hour (97 to 113kmh) when the pilot "flew the tail," easing the stick forward so the fuselage rolled level to give us a forward view. The wheels left the ground at about 100 miles per hour (161kmh). It felt like it lifted itself into the air.

Another surprise to me was the extreme noise of the engine—not like in movies, where the pilots are heard talking to each other over their microphones. It's a constant roar so loud that if I yelled to the pilot in front of me, he wouldn't hear me. If you were to fly this airplane without wearing headphones, you might damage your hearing.

Once airborne, the pilot said over the mic, "You have the airplane." There it was. The P-51 Mustang was in my hands, and I could feel everything: the slipstream moving over the control surfaces on the wings and tail, the reaction of the airplane to every little adjustment I made on the stick or rudder pedals. Right away my imagination drifted back to World War II, and I could now understand what fighter pilots felt flying the Mustang and why they liked so much. If you thought about banking to the left or right, or going up or down, it went there. After a few minutes I felt like the aircraft was an extension of my physical self, as if my mind and

Tiger Sharks of China. The 23rd Fighter Group comprised pilots from the former Flying Tigers, which were disbanded on July 4, 1942. The 23rd flew war-weary P-40s and, later, new P-40s until the summer of 1944, when they received the new P-51B and C Mustangs. American Volunteer Group ace Col. David Lee "Tex" Hill was commanding officer of the 23rd Fighter Group and was credited with fifteen-plus victories during the war. In this depiction, Tex is greeted by officers of his squadron at their base in Kweilin, China.

body had melded with this metal machine. The view out of the bubble canopy was amazing.

It took me a few minutes to get the plane flying in a level attitude, and I received two warnings about it from the pilot up front. I glanced at my vertical speed indicator and could see that I was in a very slight but steady climb. It finally dawned on me that I was using the canopy rails as visual reference to my pitch attitude, which was a bad idea since the canopy rails on the Mustang are not level, but taper downward slightly as they go forward. This is to allow the side canopy glass to be slightly lower on the forward portion to give a bit more side view looking down over the leading edge of the inboard wing sections. Always trust your instruments when your eyes aren't sure.

After that minor adjustment, I was ready to practice some maneuvers. First was a tight turn to port until the airplane returned to the initial heading, then directly into a tight turn to starboard until back to the initial heading again. I caught a quick glance at the g meter and saw 5 g during one of the turns. Not a lot, but I could feel it in my seat during the turns, which were accompanied by a slight change in engine sound and wind noise outside. I practiced other maneuvers for the next 45 minutes: roll around a point, straight rolls, split S, climbs, dives, loops, Immelmann turns. I was able to do all well after about three tries each.

After an hour of flight I set the Mustang on a heading for the airport. The pilot reminded me of approach and landing speeds and that I should plan on slowing the airplane sooner rather than later, as it is hard to slow down due to its very slippery aerodynamic shape. When I pulled the throttle back a little as we approached the airport, the plane didn't seem to slow very much.

I kept an eye on the runways and my airspeed as I got closer, trying to keep the airplane between 115 and 120 miles per hour (185 and 193kmh). On final approach there was a line of tall trees running perpendicular just before the end of the runway, and I began to sense my rate of descent would put me

below the trees before I reached the runway. Just as I was starting to push the throttle forward slowly, the pilot asked me how my approach looked. "I know I need to add little bit of power to stop my sink rate," I said, to which he replied, "Correct." I had read about flying the Mustang before flying this one and knew that it is often fatal to shove the throttle forward quickly when flying slow at low altitude because the torque of the engine will flip the aircraft upside down in a second and crash into the ground 3 seconds after that.

I pushed the throttle forward slowly and gently as I watched over the nose at the view ahead. I was still sinking below the trees but sat there and waited a couple more seconds for the engine to spool up and airspeed to increase enough to make the airplane begin to climb slightly. I cleared the trees easily and kept the airplane lined up on the center of the runway, keeping my airspeed at 110 miles per hour (177kmh), controlling the airplane's attitude and my height above the runway. The Mustang continued to descend gently

Continued on page 165

ABOVE: Pilots of the famous 332nd Fighter Group, better known as the Tuskegee Airmen, kneel in front of Capt. Andrew "Jug" Turner's P-51B/C, *Skipper's Darlin'*, at Ramitelli Air Base, Italy, in August 1944. From left: Lt. Dempsey W. Morgan Jr.; Lt. Carroll S. Woods; Lt. Robert H. Nelson Jr.; Capt. Andrew D. Turner; and Lt. Clarence P. Lester.

OPPOSITE: **Don Bryan's Big Day.** On November 2, 1944, P-51 Mustangs of the 352nd Fighter Group's 328th Squadron were involved in a large air battle over Merseberg, Germany. The squadron was credited with shooting down twenty-five enemy fighters during the engagement. Captain Don S. Bryan was flying his Mustang, *Little One III*, when he spotted a large formation of Messerschmitt Bf 109s headed for US heavy bombers. He led his flight into the Bf 109s and quickly downed five of them, making him an "ace in a day." This painting depicts Bryan downing his fifth and final victory of the combat.

ABOVE: An armorer of the 15th Air Force checks the ammunition belts for the .50-caliber machine guns in a P-51's wings before the aircraft leaves an Italian base for a mission against German military targets in September 1944. The 15th Air Force was organized for long-range assault missions.

OPPOSITE: **Alabama Rammer Jammer.** P-51D Mustang *Alabama Rammer Jammer* was flown by Arthur C. Cundy of the 352nd Fighter Squadron, 353rd Fighter Group. On January 14, 1945, Cundy's squadron was escorting US bombers of the 91st Bomb Group headed to Cologne, Germany, when Luftwaffe fighters showed up. In the ensuing battle, Cundy claimed one Fw 190 destroyed. He became an ace on March 2 but was killed on March 11 when his aircraft crashed into the English Channel.

© Jim Laurier

Continued from page 160

OPPOSITE: ***Leiston Legends.*** Charles "Chuck" Yeager and Clarence "Bud" Anderson were prominent figures in the 357th Fighter Group during World War II. On January 15, 1945, the pair took off for a "sightseeing" tour of Germany—since there had been almost no activity from the Luftwaffe for a time, it seemed like a good opportunity to log some flight time. While they were gone, the 357th got into one of its biggest air combats of the war, with many pilots raising their personal victory tallies in the "turkey shoot." In fact, the 357th downed 55.5 German aircraft in all, still a record for one day's action in the Eighth Air Force. Yeager and Anderson were not pleased when they returned to Leiston to learn they had missed all the fun.

BELOW: A murderer's row of P-51Ds photographed at the RAF's Debden base show off a variety of nose art. The P-51Ds began arriving in Europe in mid-1944.

and when I thought I felt the "ground effect" (when air can be felt compressing between the aircraft and the runway), I started to pull back slowly on the stick to make a slight flare before the wheels made contact.

"Nice landing," the pilot said. "Now go around and do it again to see if you are that good or just lucky." I pushed the throttle forward (gently, again) and we picked up speed very quickly, applying more right rudder pedal to counter the propeller torque as speed increased. In a few seconds the Mustang leapt off the ground, and I circled around for another landing, which was almost as good as the first. I heard another "Nice job" from the pilot.

The Mustang, in some ways, seemed easier to land than the lightweight Cessnas and Pipers seen at every airport. The Mustang's heavy weight, aerodynamic shape, and wide-stance landing gear make landing feel very solid, positive, and stable in all phases of the approach and procedure, including taxiing and parking.

Flying it didn't seem really difficult. Performing maneuvers was a lot of fun, and the view through the bubble canopy was unrestricted. Maneuvers beyond its normal flight envelope or beyond the ability of its pilot, however, could become disastrous very, very quickly.

It was easy for me to see why the P-51 Mustang is so loved by so many aviators around the world, past and present. I have talked to Luftwaffe pilots who fought Mustangs over Europe, and all agreed it was a wonderful fighter plane that they respected. When a Mustang was captured intact by the Germans, it was evaluated by pilots, who were surprised at its performance at all altitudes and at various power settings. Some commented they thought it was better than the Bf 109 and Fw 190. Some even remarked it may have been the best fighter plane of World War II. Some Mustangs even managed to shoot down the most advanced fighter of the war: the Me 262 jet fighter.

RIGHT: A modified P-51B serves as the first P-51D prototype in late 1942. The D became the definitive P-51 variant and notably introduced the bubble canopy to the fighter, as well as a redesigned rear fuselage and wing and a Packard-built version of the Rolls-Royce Merlin powerplant.

OPPOSITE: *The Sword and the Shield.* Ninth Tactical Air Force ace Richard "Dick" Asbury flew P-51 Mustangs during the last months of the war. The Ninth was tasked with supporting Gen. George S. Patton's armor units as they drove toward Berlin. On April 14, 1945, Asbury's flight was on patrol when they received a radio call from one of the armored units that was being strafed on a road outside of Güsten, Germany. Asbury and his wingman responded and caught a single Fw 190 making firing passes at the vehicles and troops on the ground. Asbury caught the German fighter from behind and fired a long burst from about the seven o'clock position. The Fw 190 pilot headed for a forced landing in a field, his aircraft billowing black smoke and then exploding before it reached the ground.

In an interview with Colin Heaton published in *World War II*, Luftwaffe ace Günther Rall stated:

When I was injured, I became the commander of the German Fighter Leader School for about four months or so. At that time we had formed a squadron with captured enemy aircraft, and we flew them—the P-38, P-47, P-51, as well as some Spitfires. My left hand was still in bandages, but I was flying all of these aircraft, as I was very eager to learn about and evaluate them. I had a very good impression of the P-51 Mustang, where the big difference was the engine. When we received these aircraft we flew about 300 hours in them. You see, we did not know anything about how they flew, their characteristics or anything before that. In the P-51 there was no oil leak, and that was just fantastic. This was one of the things that impressed me, but I was also very interested in the electrical starting switches, which we did not have. This made it very difficult in starting our engines in the Russian winter. We had the inertia starter. The cockpits of all of these enemy aircraft were much more comfortable. You could not fly the Bf 109 for seven hours; the cockpit was too tight, too narrow. The P-51 (cockpit) was for me a great room, just fantastic. The P-38 with two engines was great, but I think the best airplane was the P-51. Certainly the Spitfire was excellent, but it didn't have the endurance of the P-51. I think this was the decisive factor.

Today a number of P-51 Mustangs still fly, and others are in the process of being restored to flying condition. For a long time collectors have gone through great effort and expense to buy, find, and restore one of these cherished airplanes. And one that has been carefully and accurately restored can fetch two million dollars.

The Mustang had very few detracting features. If one were to try and find a fault, it may be its susceptibility to damage to its radiator located underneath the midpoint of the fuselage. Even small-arms fire could put a hole in the radiator during low-level strafing, spelling doom for the aircraft when the engine overheated and quit. But, the Mustang wasn't intended for low-level combat. No fighter fares very well from well-placed enemy rounds, no matter where they strike.

The Mustang was exactly the right aircraft at almost exactly the right time. If it had been operational a year or even six months earlier, it may have changed the course of World War II even more significantly. It is widely considered by historians and those in the aviation community to be the best fighter aircraft of World War II. In 1944, the Truman Senate War Investigating Committee rated the Mustang "the most aerodynamically perfect pursuit plane in existence." Today, among propeller-driven aircraft, it may still hold that distinction.

NORTH AMERICAN
P-51 Mustang

AIRCRAFT DEPICTED

P-51D-15-NA, S/N 44-14906 Mustang, *Cripes A'Mighty*
Flown by Major George E. "Ratsy" Preddy
328th Fighter Squadron, 352nd Fighter Group
December 1944

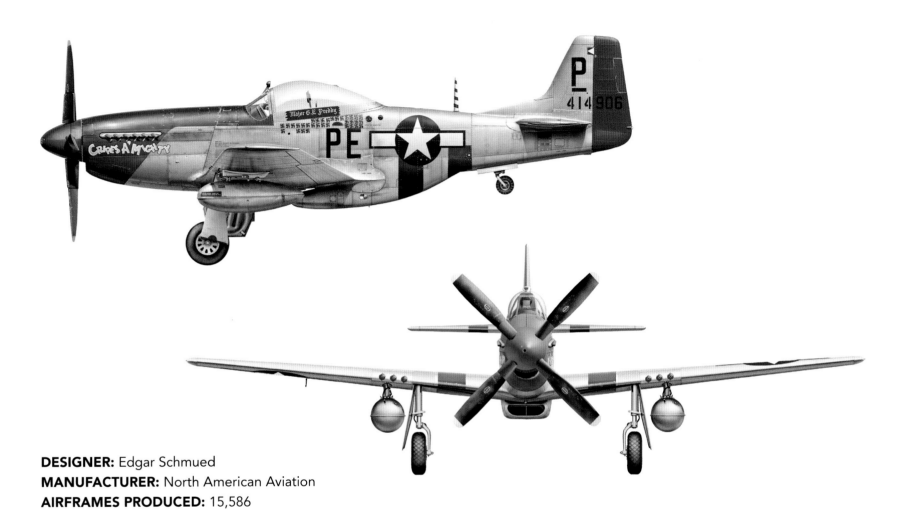

DESIGNER: Edgar Schmued
MANUFACTURER: North American Aviation
AIRFRAMES PRODUCED: 15,586

SPECIFICATIONS

Length . . . . 32 ft 2 in (9.80m)

Wingspan . . . . 37 ft 4 in (11.38m)

Height . . . . 13 ft 6 in (4.11m)

Empty weight . . . . 9,611 lb (4,360kg)

Loaded weight . . . . .12,100 lb (5,489kg)

Engine . . . . Rolls-Royce/Packard
V-1650-7 liquid-cooled V-12

Output . . . . 1,490 hp

Maximum speed . . . . 437 mph (700kmh)

Cruising speed. . . . . 325 mph (523kmh)

Landing speed . . . . 111 mph (179kmh)

Ceiling . . . . 36,900 ft (11,890m)

Range . . . . 2,393 mi (3,851km) with drop tanks

Armament . . . . 50-caliber machine guns × 6

NORTH AMERICAN
P-51 Mustang

1. Landing gear control lever
2. Elevator trim tab control wheel
3. Carburetor hot air control lever
4. Carburetor cold air control lever
5. Rudder trim tab control
6. Aileron trim tab control
7. Radiator air control (coolant)
8. Radiator air control (oil)
9. Landing light switch
10. Fluorescent light switch (left)
11. Flare pistol mount cover cap
12. Arm rest
13. Mixture control lever
14. Throttle quadrant locks
15. Throttle lever
16. Propeller control lever
17. Selector dimmer assembly
18. Instrument light
19. Rear warning radar lamp
20. K-14A gunsight
21. Laminated glass
22. Remote compass indicator
23. Clock
24. Suction gauge
25. Manifold pressure gauge
26. Airspeed indicator
27. Directional gyro turn indicator
28. Artificial horizon
29. Coolant temperature
30. Tachometer
31. Altimeter
32. Turn and bank indicator
33. Rate of climb indicator
34. Carburetor air temperature

35. Engine T gauge
36. Bomb salvo release lever(s)
37. Engine control panel
38. Landing gear warning light(s)
39. Parking brake handle
40. Oxygen flow blinker
41. Oxygen pressure gauge
42. Ignition switch
43. Bomb and rocket switch
44. Cockpit light control
45. Rocket control panel
46. Fuel shutoff valve
47. Fuel selector valve
48. Emergency hydraulic
    release handle
49. Hydraulic pressure gauge
50. Oxygen hose
51. Oxygen regulator
52. Emergency canopy
    release handle
53. Canopy crank and lock handle
54. IFF control panel
55. IFF detonator button(s)
56. VHF radio control box
57. Rear warning radar control panel
58. VHF volume control knob
59. Fluorescent light switch (right)
60. Electrical control panel
61. Circuit breakers
62. BC-438 control box
63. Cockpit light
64. Circuit breakers
65. Rudder pedals
66. Control column
67. Flap controls lever
68. Pilot's seat
69. Flare gun storage

CHAPTER 10

MESSERSCHMITT
Me 262

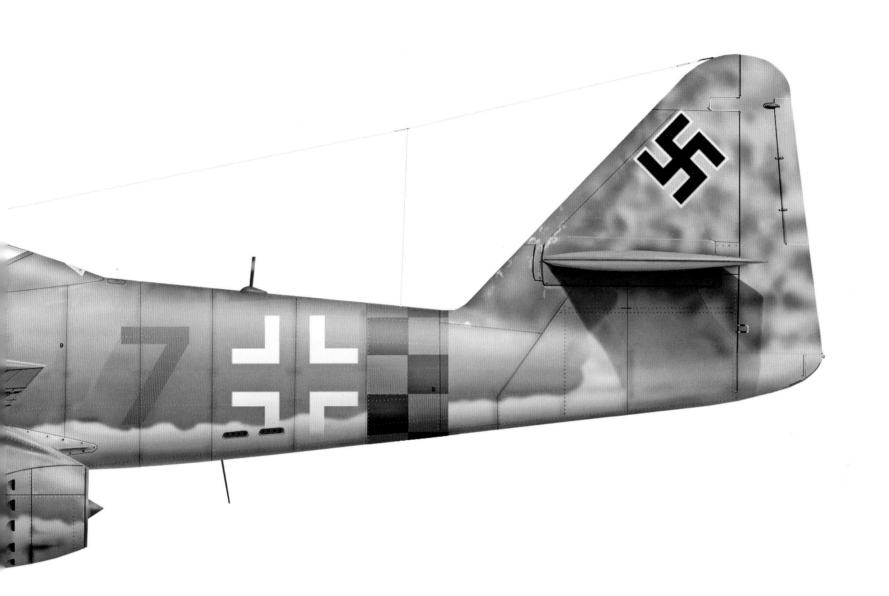

The Messerschmitt Me 262 was not the first jet fighter in history, but it became famous as the first combat-operational jet fighter in early 1944. In Britain, Frank Whittle had been working on his jet engine designs since 1935, but the first RAF jet fighter, the Gloster Meteor, was not ready for operations until July 1944.

The development of jet-powered aircraft was not given priority at the beginning of the war because the major powers were already committed to developing and producing the many piston-powered fighter and bomber aircraft that were tested and proven weapons of the time. The idea of jet propulsion had not yet taken root in the minds of most military leaders, and the prospect of spending wartime resources developing jet-powered aircraft seemed unnecessary, if not outright foolish, when aircraft already being produced were proving effective.

There were, however, a few key figures in the Luftwaffe who saw some promise in the concept. In 1938 the German Air Ministry (RLM) announced a turbojet design competition. The two main competitors were Heinkel and Messerschmitt.

Each design team had an idea for what they thought the Luftwaffe needed to win the war in the skies over Europe, but Messerschmitt would eventually win favor with the Luftwaffe, largely due to the fact the firm had already produced a number of winning bomber and fighter designs for Germany. The RLM assigned the designation Me 262 to the new jet design, which was called the Schwalbe (Swallow).

Two annoying obstacles stood before Willy Messerschmitt. One was the director general of equipment, who, for some reason, did not like Messerschmitt and did everything possible to thwart the progress of the Me 262. The other was the slow development of the jet engines Messerschmitt needed. Certain crucial alloys were unavailable in Germany in sufficient quantities and had to be imported, which was difficult and time-consuming during wartime.

When the first prototype airframe was ready for testing in 1941, rather than holding up progress waiting for the jet engines, Messerschmitt installed a single 700-horsepower Junkers Jumo 210G piston engine to airframe Me 262V-1 so he could get it airborne for initial flight testing.

The first flight occurred on April 18, 1941, with good results, although the aircraft was underpowered. On November 25, 1941, Me 262V-1 had two BMW 003 turbojet engines added to its wings and flew with these plus a Jumo piston engine. Both jet engines failed after takeoff, and the pilot managed to land safely with just the piston engine. On July 18, 1942, Me 262V-3 flew for the first time with the Junkers Jumo

R-Bar over Bielefeld. On November 2, 1944, B-24s of the 489th Bomb Group were sent to destroy the railroad marshaling yards at Bielefeld, Germany. The bombers were met by the new German jet fighter, the Messerschmitt Me 262, in one of the earliest jet attacks against US bombers. The Me 262's high closing speed made it impossible for the jets to hit anything, and they were chased off by escorting P-47s after one firing pass.

PREVIOUS PAGES: Me 262A-1a Schwalbe flown by Oberfeldwebel Franz Gapp, VIII./KG(J) 6, May 1945.

004A-0 jet engines, as originally intended. These engines were more reliable and provided 1,850 pounds of thrust each, enough to make the jet perform as projected.

There was still doubt among some in the RLM about the future of the Me 262, so Messerschmitt enlisted the help of one of the Luftwaffe's most respected pilots, Adolf Galland, who demonstrated the Me 262's abilities to the RLM and top Luftwaffe officers. Still, no production orders resulted. The first five prototypes had been taildraggers, but on November 26, 1943, the first nose wheel–equipped Me 262V-6 was demonstrated for Adolf Hitler, who was pleased with the new jet. Unfortunately, Hitler also saw the jet fighter as a fast bomber and ordered its production to proceed as such, providing one more example of bad decisions from Hitler that helped ensure Germany's defeat.

In a bold move, and with the support of many in the upper ranks of the Luftwaffe, Messerschmitt went ahead with the production of the Me 262 as a fighter. Hitler learned of this in May 1944 and, in a rage, again ordered the jets to be produced strictly as bombers. This, along with a shortage of Jumo 004B engines, delayed production for about six more months. By then, Hitler had been partially convinced to allow the jet aircraft to be produced in both the fighter and bomber configurations, with the mandate that the bomber version be capable of carrying at least one 250-pound bomb.

Formal production began in May 1944 with the Me 262A-1, which had four nose-mounted 30-millimeter Mk 108 cannons. One of the early preproduction models was specially streamlined and reached a top speed of 624 miles per hour (1,004kmh), but the modification was not incorporated into regular production for some reason. Me 262A-2s were fitted with bomb pylons to carry two 500-pound bombs or one 100-pound bomb. The two upper Mk 108 guns were removed on this variant. Jumo B-1, B-2, and B-3 engines were used.

Many new aircraft designs in World War II underwent numerous trial modifications to gain some advantage or to fill specific roles. The Germans were the premier innovators in this respect and tried several modifications with the Me 262, some appearing strange, others slightly more sensible. The Me 262 A-1a/R1 carried twenty-four rockets on the wings, which proved effective in bringing down heavy bombers. Four Me 262A-1s had a single 50-millimeter Mk 214 nose-mounted cannon that extended 7 feet (2.1m) ahead of the nose, but this proved too impractical and ineffective. Other modified versions included:

- **Me 262A-1a/U2:** Fitted with FuG 220 Lichtenstein SN-2 90-megahertz radar transceiver and Hirschgeweih antenna array
- **Me 262A-1a/U3:** Unarmed recon version with two downward-pointing nose-mounted *Reihenbilder* RB 50/30 cameras
- **Me 262 A-1a/U5:** Heavy jet fighter with six 30-millimeter Mk 108s in the nose
- **Me 262A-2a:** *Sturmvogel* fighter-bomber armed as 1a with 1,000kg bomb load

ABOVE: A Me 262a-1a of III./EJG 2 taxis for another training sortie early November 1944. III./EJG2 was the official training establishment for all future Me 262 fighter pilots.

OPPOSITE: *Night Hawk.* In this fictional scene an ultra-rare Me 262B-1a/U1 night fighter leaves the airfield for a night-training flight. This aircraft was equipped with FuG 218 radar in the nose, which was operated by a pilot in the rear seat. Very few of these variants were produced, with even fewer becoming operational, those serving with 10./NJG 11.

- **Me 262A-2a/U2:** Featured a bulged glazed wooden nose that housed a second crewmember lying prone and using a Lotfe 7H bombsight
- **Me 262A-3a:** Proposed ground-attack version armed as 1a with extra armor for the fuel tanks, floor, and cockpit sidewalls
- **Me 262A-5a:** Recon fighter with two 30-millimeter Mk 108 cannons and two RB 50/30 vertically mounted cameras in the nose with an observation panel in the floor of the cockpit and pylons for two 66-gallon or one 132-gallon external tank
- **Me 262B-1:** Twin-seat trainer armed as 1a with internal fuel reduced and replaced with

two 66-gallon or one 132-gallon external tank; fifteen produced
- **Me 262B-1a/U1:** Two-seat night fighter armed as 1a with FuG 218, 120a, and FuG 350 ZC "Naxos"
- **Me 262B-2a:** Fuselage lengthened 3 feet 11¼ inches (1.2m) with increased 257-gallon fuel capacity armed as 1a with two additional remote-controlled Mk 108 cannons with Schräge Musik installation with FuG 350 ZC "Naxos"
- **Me 262C-1a:** Armed as 1a with Walter HWK (109-509) rocket in tail
- **Me 262C-2b:** Armed as 1a with two 1,760-pounds-force BMW 003R engines

Heinz Bär. Oskar-Heinz "Pritzl" Bär was a 220-victory ace with the Luftwaffe in World War II. Bär began flying the Me 262 with the III./ EJG 2 training unit in February 1945. In April he transferred to the elite jet unit JG 44. While flying the Me 262, Bär downed thirteen enemy aircraft. Some of his final victories on April 27 and 28 were P-47 Thunderbolts.

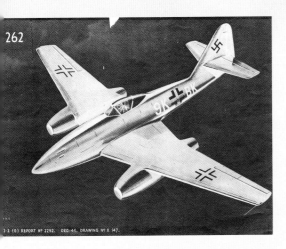

This Air Intelligence (AI) illustration of the Me 262 fighter was widely distributed to all Allied fighter squadrons in December 1944. The Me 262 entered service in small numbers beginning August 1944.

combined with 3-minute-duration 2,700-pounds-force BMW 718 bi-fuel rocket motor; only one flight test made

- **Me 262C-3:** Proposed version with a jettisonable Walter rocket motor fed by a jettisonable fuel tank forward of the rocket motor, both located under the fuselage
- **Me 262D:** Proposed version with the SG 500 *Jagdfaust* comprising twelve rifled mortar barrels in the nose, pointing forward and upward
- **Me 262E-2:** Proposed version with twelve R4M rockets on each wing and twenty-four R4M rockets in the nose

By some accounts, 1,433 Me 262s had been built by war's end. Some estimate that over one-third were destroyed on the ground by Allied bombing raids and strafing.

After the war, a small number of Me 262s were built in Prague, Czechoslovakia, by Avia, nine as single-seat S-92s and three as two-seat CS-92s. The Czechoslovak Air Force operated them until 1951.

Many Me 262s were captured by Allies at the end of World War II and closely studied. The secrets they revealed paved the way for jet aircraft designs that followed, and many of their features are still present in their basic forms in jet aircraft of today.

★ ★ ★

The jet age was inevitable. It was still quite a shock, and probably a bit thrilling, when the first Me 262 jet fighter met Allied aircraft in the skies over Germany. Nearly 100 miles per hour (160kmh) faster than the fastest piston-powered fighter of the war, it could sweep through bomber formations with incredible speed, giving little opportunity for gunners to even identify it, let alone get a shot at it.

What was it? Some fliers had heard rumors about a new German jet and surmised they had just seen one

flash by their aircraft. Others had no idea what it was and reported they thought they had seen some kind of fighter plane with no propeller. Soon enough they realized a new form of advanced fighter was after them, and it was terrifying to imagine how they would be able to defend themselves against it.

The first encounter between US bombers and Me 262s was thought to be on November 2, 1944, when B-24s of the 489th Bomber Group were heading to Bielefeld, Germany. Lead bombers in the formation could see fighters circling around high above and in front of them. Suddenly, the fighters came down straight at them and had flown past in a second, offering a brief glimpse, just enough to identify them as the new jets. Their closing speed was so fast the jets managed to fire only a few rounds before being chased off by escorting P-47 Thunderbolts.

Thus the Luftwaffe realized one of the Me 262s weaknesses: its speed. The very thing that was its greatest asset could also be a hindrance. The jet was so fast there was little time to sight and fire with any accuracy. The jets' cannons had a slow rate of fire and were only accurate at relatively close range, which allowed insufficient time to hit anything before they had to break away to avoid colliding with the bombers.

Tactics quickly changed to attacks from the rear of bomber formations, but even this allowed only 2 or 3 seconds to gain accurate sighting and fire. Many modifications began appearing on the jets in an effort to find ways to attack bombers. One of the most effective was the Me 262A-1a/R1, which had twenty-four rockets that could be fired from an oblique lateral deflection angle at long range. The rockets were aimed to fan out in a boxed array, and only one or two hits from any of these approximately 50-pound projectiles was sufficient to bring down a bomber.

The other major shortcoming in the Me 262's design was the new jet engines themselves. Temperatures generated could be as high as 1,800 degrees Fahrenheit, requiring special metals and metal alloys to withstand such

ABOVE: In addition to the fighter version, the Me 262 was produced as a fighter-bomber, night-fighter, and photo-reconnaissance aircraft. This is an Me 262a-1a *Jabo* fighter-bomber (note the bomb pylons under the forward fuselage).

OPPOSITE: **Me 262 over Keene.** In this fictitious scene, an Me 262A flies over Dillant Hopkins airport in Keene, New Hampshire. This is where I live and the airport is where I received my flight training. The region is on almost the same latitude as parts of Germany, and from the air there are lots of similarities in scenery, so the camouflage colors on the jet are effective against the background terrain.

high temperatures. These alloys were available only in small quantities, and the time needed to import sufficient amounts drastically slowed production. The decision was made to use more conventional metals like steel and aluminum instead. As a result, the maximum number of hours the Jumo 004 engines could safely be operated was set at 25 hours before they had to be replaced. This was not the best solution, but one the Luftwaffe could live with, given the options. The Me 262 was designed so that an engine could be replaced in roughly an hour.

Throttle lag time was another of the Me 262's undesirable realities. The new Jumo turbojet engines could not respond quickly to aggressive throttle inputs. The throttle had to be used with care; the pilot couldn't floor it to accelerate, especially at lower speeds. To gain speed, the throttle had to be pushed forward slowly to let the engine spool up to higher rpms. Speed would increase quickly and steadily, but not instantly. This problem made the jets very vulnerable to attack during landing and takeoff, and many were caught this way and shot down in the airfield pattern while low and slow.

On the plus side, the speed of the Me 262 was the thing its pilots loved the most. They didn't care how many times the engines had to be replaced, as long as

© Jim Laurier

they could fly the aircraft. Another positive thing pilots noticed was the lack of deafening engine noise in the cockpit. Radio communications could be heard more easily, and there was no need to yell into the mic. I have flown in both jet- and piston-powered fighters, and the difference is like night and day. A piston-powered fighter creates a steady and constant engine roar, with only slight variations depending on the maneuvers being performed. In a jet, there is almost no vibration, and the slight sound of the rushing air of the slipstream passing over the aircraft makes the flight seem much more comfortable.

Once pilots were properly trained and could master the Me 262, they could control the skies. The aircraft had a reputation of being a bit cantankerous and difficult to fly at times, but that was an acceptable tradeoff for those who were confident in their flying skills. Most pilots who flew Me 262s in combat were specially selected and highly skilled Luftwaffe veterans. Estimates vary as to how many Me 262s actually saw

combat, ranging from as few as one hundred to as many as three hundred. At any one time, only about fifty or so were operational.

Still, the Me 262 is credited with destroying more than five hundred Allied aircraft during its brief reign, compared to a loss of about 100 to 120 of their own. That five-to-one kill ratio is an impressive record in any era.

When interviewing Luftwaffe ace Gen. Adolf Galland, I asked what it was like to fly the Me 262. He responded that its best feature was its speed and that he felt it handled very well with a responsive feel at the controls. He added the radio equipment was good, and it was a great weapons platform, having a closely grouped array of heavy-hitting cannons in the nose. He thought that, all things considered, it was like flying any other fighter in that once a pilot had learned how to best use it, he could be successful with it. Of course, what he loved most was its speed, which

BELOW LEFT: The Me 262a-1a *Jabo* was capable of carrying two 1,100-pound (500kg) bombs. Armed with four Mk 108 30-millimeter cannons grouped in the nose, the Me 262 was well-equipped for the bomber-interceptor and ground-attack roles.

BELOW: A Messerschmitt Me 262 (Werknummer 111711) on a tarmac somewhere in the United States. On March 31, 1945, this aircraft became the first intact Me 262 to fall into Allied hands.

A captured Jumo 004 jet engine is examined at the Aircraft Engine Research Laboratory of the National Advisory Committee for Aeronautics, Cleveland, Ohio, in 1946.

changed the air war. It would most certainly not have changed the final outcome of the war, for we had already lost completely, but it would have probably delayed the end, since the Normandy invasion on June 6, 1944, would probably not have taken place, at least not successfully if the 262 had been operational. I certainly think that just 300 jets flown daily by the best fighter pilots would have had a major impact on the course of the air war. This would have, of course, prolonged the war, so perhaps Hitler's misuse of this aircraft was not such a bad thing after all.

The misuse was, of course, Hitler's decision to use the jet as a bomber, a task it was not designed to perform. In my conversations with Luftwaffe officers over the years, all agreed that many of Hitler's decisions did as much to defeat Germany as other factors.

It is estimated that, during their brief reign, Me 262s destroyed around five hundred Allied aircraft, most of them bombers. The jet fighter's most notable statistic is its air combat kill ratio of 5:1—an impressive feat in any era.

At war's end, a number of German aircraft were sought out for testing and evaluation, with the Me 262 at the top of the list. A special team headed by Col. H. E. Watson was organized for gathering these aircraft and getting them flightworthy and shipped back to the United States. Many US and British pilots had the opportunity to fly variants of the Me 262, and their conclusions were unanimous: it was the most amazing thing they had ever flown.

Pilots who flew the Me 262, as well as all top Allied officers and leaders, suddenly realized how important this jet fighter was, not only to the course of World War II, but to the future of fighter aircraft. The Me 262 was the technological blueprint to all future jet aircraft. Like a bright comet, the Me 262 lit up the skies for a brief time and, in the process, ignited the imaginations of the next generation of aeronautical engineers.

offered the pilot the ability to attack or escape quickly when necessary.

In fighter pilot parlance, speed is life, and altitude is insurance. The Me 262 certainly had both. Typical top speed was around 540 miles per hour (870kmh), and it could climb over 37,000 feet (11,280m) quickly. Had this jet been put into production sooner strictly as a defensive fighter, as Willy Messerschmitt had intended, Allied bomber losses could possibly have soared to unsustainable levels.

In an article that appeared in a 1997 issue of *World War II* magazine, Colin Heaton quoted Galland:

> I believe the 262 could have been made operational as a fighter at least a year and a half earlier and built in large enough numbers so that it could have

MESSERSCHMITT
Me 262

AIRCRAFT DEPICTED

Me 262A-1

Flown by Leutnant Franz Schall

Kommando Nowotny

Achmer, Germany

October 28, 1944

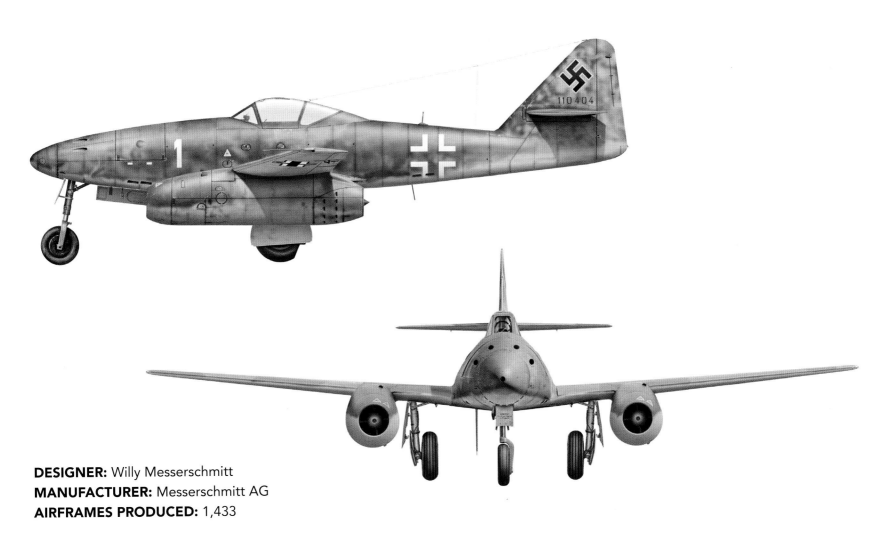

DESIGNER: Willy Messerschmitt
MANUFACTURER: Messerschmitt AG
AIRFRAMES PRODUCED: 1,433

SPECIFICATIONS

Length . . . . 34 ft 8 in (10.57m)

Wingspan . . . . 41 ft 6 in (12.60m)

Height . . . . 11 ft 6 in (3.51m)

Empty weight . . . . 8,378 lb (3,800kg)

Loaded weight . . . . .14,110 lb (6,400kg)

Engines . . . . Junkers Jumo 004B-1 × 2

Output. . . . . 1,978 ft-lb thrust × 2

Max speed. . . . . 559 mph (900kmh)

Cruising speed. . . . . 460 mph (740kmh)

Ceiling . . . . 37,565 ft (11,450m)

Range . . . . 652 mi (1,050km)

Armament . . . . .30mm Mk 108 cannons × 4

MESSERSCHMITT Me 262

1. Airspeed indicator
2. Artificial horizon
3. Variometer
4. Altimeter
5. Radio compass
6. SZKK-2 ammunition counter
7. Tachometers
8. Exhaust gas temperature gauges
9. Fuel-injection pressure gauges
10. Fuel gauges
11. Cockpit heat control
12. Fuel counters
13. Engine starter switches
14. Gun camera switch
15. Free air temperature gauge
16. Hydraulic pressure gauge
17. Nose wheel brake
18. Ventilator control
19. Vertical speed indicator
20. Turn and bank indicator
21. Oil pressure gauge
22. AFN-2 indicator

23. Clock
24. REVI 16B Gun sight
25. Oxygen flow meter
26. Oxygen contents gauge
27. Emergency landing-gear handle
28. Emergency flaps handle
29. Horizontal stabilizer trim control
30. Horizontal stabilizer trim indicator
31. Landing gear indicator lights
32. Fuel shutoff selector lever
33. Throttle controls
34. Oxygen control valve
35. Main light switch
36. Rudder pedals
37. Control column
38. Pilot's seat
39. Canopy release lever
40. Switches panel
41. Windshield heater switch
42. Flare release switch
43. Bomb release handle
44. Bomb control panel
45. Circuit breaker test panel
46. FuG 25 IFF panel

IMAGE CREDITS

All artwork © Jim Laurier except as noted below.

The artworks on the following pages appear courtesy of **Osprey Publishing**: 28; 42; 60; 64–65; 76; 94; 104; 114; 121; 130; 139; 148; 161; 170. **Creative Commons, Bundesarchiv, Bild 1011-487-3066-04/Boyer/CC-BY-SA**: 16. **Donald Nijboer Collection**: 176; 179; 180; 182 (left). **Kure Maritime Museum**: 67; 68. **Library of Congress**: 23. **Library of Congress, Office of War Information**: 85 (top); 89 (left); 90; 101; 123 (left); 123 (right); 127 (right); 156. **National Aeronautics and Space Administration (NASA)**: 37; 73; 83 (right); 120; 154; 155; 183. **National Archives and Records Administration**: 50; 89 (right); 100; 157; 160; 162. **National Museum of the USAF**: 15 (top). **Public Domain**: 19; 21 (top); 21 (bottom); 22; 25; 37; 66; 70 (left); 70 (right); 83 (left); 104; 106; 107 (left). **Royal Canadian Air Force**: 35. **United States Air Force**: 48; 49; 54; 55; 57; 82 (left and right); 86 (top); 107 (right); 124; 127 (left); 136; 139; 141; 142 (top); 145 (left); 145 (right); 165; 167; 182 (right). **United States Air Force via Mark Donaghue**: 51; 53 (top); 88; 142 (left). **US Navy Naval History and Heritage Command**: 103 (top).

INDEX

First published in 2016 by Voyageur Press, an imprint of Quarto Publishing Group USA Inc., 400 First Avenue North, Suite 400, Minneapolis, MN 55401 USA. Telephone: (612) 344-8100 Fax: (612) 344-8692

quartoknows.com
Visit our blogs at quartoknows.com

Voyageur Press titles are also available at discounts in bulk quantity for industrial or sales-promotional use. For details contact the Special Sales Manager at Quarto Publishing Group USA Inc., 400 First Avenue North, Suite 400, Minneapolis, MN 55401 USA.

No artwork in this book may be reproduced in any form without written consent from the artist. Some images may be available for purchase as limited-edition art prints or canvas giclée prints. For inquiries, please visit www.jimlaurier.com, contact the artist by email at jlaurier@ne.rr.com, or write to:

Jim Laurier
PO Box 1118
Keene, NH 03431
USA

10 9 8 7 6 5 4 3 2 1

ISBN: 978-0-7603-4952-6

Library of Congress Cataloging-in-Publication Data

Names: Laurier, Jim.
Title: Fighter! : ten killer planes of World War II / Jim Laurier.
Description: Minneapolis, MN : Voyageur Press, 2016. | Includes index.
Identifiers: LCCN 2016019275 | ISBN 9780760349526 (plc w/jacket)
Subjects: LCSH: World War, 1939-1945--Aerial operations. | Fighter
    planes--History--20th century.
Classification: LCC D785 .L38 2016 | DDC 940.54/4--dc23
LC record available at https://lccn.loc.gov/2016019275

Acquiring Editors: Elizabeth Demers, Dennis Pernu
Project Manager: Madeleine Vasaly
Art Director: James Kegley
Cover Designer: Karl Laun
Layout: Kim Winscher

Printed in China